Welcome

It is always our great pleasure to welcome all visitors to Pembrokeshire, and we hope that you can use our guide to maximise your stay. Pembrokeshire is a county steeped in history, myths and legends through the centuries. The evidence of the sweeping changes throughout Pembrokeshire are evident everywhere you look, from drowned prehistoric forests, to Iron Age Forts and Bronze Age burial chambers. We hope that this guide will serve a very practical purpose during your stay with its maps and multiple guides. After your stay you will be able to take the time, sit back and read through all the background information about the places that you visited. We genuinely hope that you enjoy your visit to our beautiful county and that you can use our guide to get the most out of your holiday.

Please enjoy your stay.

GW00727888

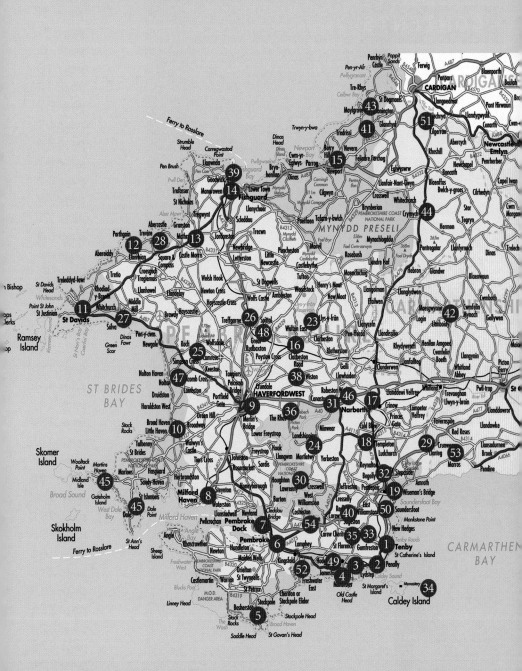

CONTENTS

PEMBROKESHIRE BEACH GUIDE

Pembrokeshire is truly blessed with some of the most stunning beaches in the country. Offering delights from the ever popular beaches at Saundersfoot and Tenby to the secluded magic of sandy stretches at the likes of Barafundle and Whitesands. If you are more of an active persuasion, please see our activities section for the best beaches for water based sports.

Life's a Beach

Blue Flags are the European standard for quality beaches with excellent water quality and a good range of facilities such as toilets.

Seaside awards are a U.K. only scheme for beaches with at least good water quality but they may not have all facilities needed for a Blue Flag award.

Green Coast awards are for isolated rural beaches with excellent water quality but few or no facilities

Look out for these flags, they mark bathing areas patrolled by life guards.

Two black & white flags mark non swimming areas zoned mainly for surfing, windsurfing or a motorised craft beach access point.

Take note of this flag, it indicates dangerous conditions, DO NOT GO SWIMMING when it's flying.

All awards shown have been applied for the 2011 season

WATER QUALITY:
E = EXCELLENT G = GOOD
NT = NOT TESTED

Lifeguards & Beach attendants on duty from the last week in June to the first weekend in September 10am to 6pm daily

Please take note of the flags (ask the lifeguards if you're in doubt) and ensure that everyone has a happy - and safe - day at the beach!

Beach	Description	Water Quality	Dog Restriction
ST. DOGMAELS	M F E	NT	NF
POPPIT	S D	E	NF
CEIBWR	R S	NT	NF
NEWPORT SANDS	S D	E	NF
NEWPORT PARROG	E S R	NT	NF
CWM-YR-EGLWYS	S ST RP	E	NF
PWLL GWAELOD	S SH	NT	NF
LOWER FISHGUARD	H	NT	NF
GOODWICK SANDS	S ST	E	NF
ABERBACH (ST. NICHOLAS)	P S C	NT	NF
ABERMAWR	P S R	E	NF
ABERCASTLE	R C SH	E	NF
ABERFELIN/TREFIN	SH R C	NT	NF
PORTHGAIN	H	NT	NF
TRAETHLLYFN	S R C RP	NT	NF
ABEREIDDY	S R C RP	E	NF
PORTHMELGEN	C R S	NT	NF
WHITESANDS	S ST R	E	NF
PORTHSELAU	R S C	E	NF
PORTHCLAIS	H	NT	NF
CAERFAI	S C R	E	NF
SOLVA	H	NT	NF
NEWGALE	P S C ST	E	NF
NOLTON HAVEN	C S ST R	G	NF
DRUIDSTON	C S P ST	E	NF
BROAD HAVEN	S P ST R	E	NF
LITTLE HAVEN	S ST R	E	NF
ST. BRIDES HAVEN	R S ST	E	NF
MARTINS HAVEN	R P	E	NF
MARLOES SANDS	S C R	E	NF
WEST DALE	S C R	E	NF
DALE	P S R ST	E	NF
LINDSWAY BAY	S R	NT	NF
SANDY HAVEN	C R S	G	NF
GELLISWICK	S R	G	NF
LLANSTADWELL	S E	NT	X NF
NEYLAND	SH MF	NT	X NF
BURTON	E	NT	X NF
LLANGWM/BLACKTAR	E SH	NT	X NF
LAWRENNY	E SH MF	NT	NF
EAST LLANION	E	E	X NF
ANGLE BAY	E MF	NT	NF
WEST ANGLE BAY	R S	G	NF
FRESHWATER WEST	S R ST D	E	BEWARE OF STRONG RIP CURRENTS — NF
BROAD HAVEN SOUTH	S D ST	E	NF
BARAFUNDLE BAY	S D ST	E	NF
STACKPOLE QUAY	H	NT	NF
FRESHWATER EAST	S D ST	E	NF
MANORBIER	S D ST	E	NF
LYDSTEP HAVEN	S SH	E	X NF
PENALLY	S D	E	NF
PRIORY BAY CALDEY	S	E	NF
TENBY SOUTH	S D	E	NF
TENBY CASTLE	S	E	NF
TENBY HARBOUR	H	NT	NF
TENBY NORTH	S	E	NF
MONKSTONE	S R	E	NF
GLEN BEACH	S R	G	NF
SAUNDERSFOOT	S H	E	NF
COPPET HALL	S R	E	NF
WISEMANS BRIDGE	S R	G	NF
AMROTH	S R	G	NF

Beach Description Key

S SAND BEACH	P PEBBLE BEACH	ST STREAM	R ROCKY	RP ROCK POOLS	E ESTUARY
D SAND DUNES	C CLIFFS	SH SHINGLE	MF MUD FLATS	H HARBOUR	X PONTOON

NF NO DOG FOULING - PICK UP AFTER YOUR DOG. CONSIDER OTHER BEACH USERS

Water Quality gradings: **EXCELLENT** = complies with the E.C. Guideline standard. **GOOD** = complies with the mandatory standard. Beaches that are not tested are generally smaller, adjacent to tested beaches or in isolated locations.

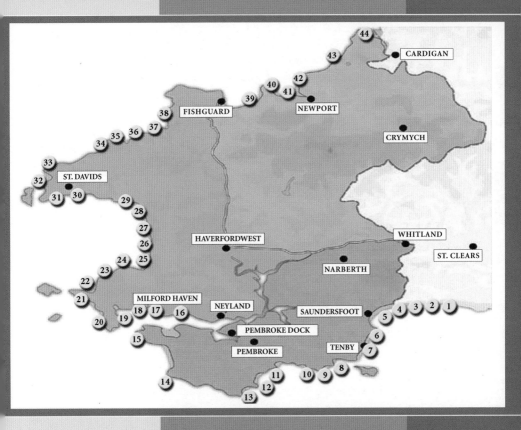

Map labels: 44, 43, CARDIGAN, 42, 40, 41, 39, NEWPORT, 38, FISHGUARD, 37, 36, 35, 34, CRYMYCH, 33, 32, ST. DAVIDS, 31, 30, 29, 28, 27, 26, WHITLAND, HAVERFORDWEST, ST. CLEARS, 24, 25, 23, NARBERTH, 22, 21, MILFORD HAVEN, 18, 17, 16, NEYLAND, SAUNDERSFOOT, 5, 4, 3, 2, 1, 20, 19, 6, 15, PEMBROKE DOCK, 7, PEMBROKE, TENBY, 11, 10, 9, 8, 14, 12, 13

SOUTH COAST

It is no surprise that many visitors to Pembrokeshire come here first and foremost for the county's magnificent sandy beaches. Our counties beaches are regular award winners throughout the years, please check page 6 of this guide for this year's up to date information. So whether you are a sun worshipper, watersports fanatic, boat owner or you simply love the seaside, Pembrokeshire is an idyllic place to enjoy the great beach holiday.

AMROTH (1)

Amroth is a charming coastal village where time seems to have stood still. The beach is punctuated by a series of groynes that help protect the village from winter storms and rough seas. The Western end marks the start of the renowned 186 mile Pembrokeshire Coastal Path. Parking is good along the seafront and in the village.

Amroth

Amroth

Coppet Hall

WISEMANS BRIDGE (2)

The beach's claim to fame is that it was used in 1944 for rehearsals of the D Day landings under the watchful eye of Sir Winston Churchill himself. The beach is sandy and it's possible to walk to neighbouring Saundersfoot at low tide. Parking is limited.

COPPET HALL (3)

Coppet Hall is a popular beach which has extensive parking facilities. It also affords access to Saundersfoot village.

SAUNDERSFOOT (4)

Saundersfoot is one of the area's most popular resorts and it's easy to see why. There is everything for the family including a superb beach and a range of shops, cafes and restaurants. There is also a picturesque harbour plus extensive parking facilities.

MONKSTONE (5)

Monkstone (Saundersfoot) is unsuitable for families as access is down very steep steps. Those hardy enough to

Tenby

make the journey will find a beautiful stretch of sand but no facilities. Entry to the beach is through Trevayne Farm off the B4316 near New Hedges. There is a small charge for parking.

TENBY NORTH (6)

Tenby is one of the most popular seaside resorts in Wales. A medieval walled town with narrow streets, it stands on a rocky headland which divides its two main beaches. The award winning North Beach has first class facilities together with a picture postcard harbour and sandy beach. Because of the town's narrow streets, visitors are advised to park in one of the large car parks outside the town walls, all of which are within walking distance of the beaches.

TENBY SOUTH (7)

Tenby's South Beach offers a large expanse of fine sand. A firm favourite with people holidaying at the nearby Kiln Park Holiday Village. The beach, which is backed by cliffs on which the town stands, offers unlimited views of Caldey Island which is inhabited by monks. Facilities are excellent.

Tenby

Saundersfoot

LYDSTEP HAVEN (8)

Lydstep Haven is a privately owned beautiful sheltered bay for which there is an admission charge. Characterised at either end by wooded cliffs, Lydstep boasts a slipway to cater for the many boats and pleasure crafts using the bay. One of the area's main features is the Smugglers Cave, which can be explored even at high tide.

SKRINKLE HAVEN (9)

Skrinkle Haven is an absolute gem of a beach sheltered by tall cliffs. However, there is no access to the public. There is a car park above the beach but no other facilities.

MANORBIER (10)

Manorbier is very popular with surfers. Overlooked by a medieval castle and the 12th Century church of St James, the beach is the home to a stone cromlech known as the King's Quoit. The sandy beach is served by a large car park, together with parking areas on the road above the beach.

FRESHWATER EAST (11)

Freshwater East is a wide, sweeping crescent of sand and shingle backed by dunes and grassy headlands. Popular with boat owners, divers, fishermen and surfers.

Freshwater West

BARAFUNDLE (12)

Barafundle is surely one of Pembrokeshire's most beautiful beaches, it is however only accessible from the coastal path. Owned by the National Trust, the nearest parking is at Stackpole Quay about half a mile away. Due to its remote location the beach itself has no amenities, but there is a tearoom at Stackpole Quay.

BROAD HAVEN SOUTH (13)

Broad Haven South is a superb sheltered beach popular with sun worshipers. Another of the National Trust owned beaches, it offers excellent parking for both those visiting the beach or those using it as a gateway to the area's many fine walks.

FRESHWATER WEST (14)

Freshwater West is a haven for surfers. They are drawn to the area by the big Atlantic rollers so it seems only natural that the beach has been used for the Welsh National Surfing Championships. However, it can be dangerous to swimmers because of strong rip currents and hazardous quicksands so families with small children should be on their guard.

Freshwater East

Barafundle

9

Dale

West
Angle Bay

WEST COAST

WEST ANGLE BAY (15)

West Angle Bay is another beautiful location, very popular with visitors and local inhabitants alike. Low tides reveal rock pools, which youngsters can explore. The beach houses the remains of an old lime kiln now partly overgrown. There are excellent walks along the cliffs offering spectacular views. Parking and other facilities are good.

GELLISWICK (16)

Gelliswick is the headquarters of the Pembrokeshire Yacht Club and offers an excellent slipway for boats. A large sand and shingle beach, facilities include toilets, free parking and the nearby shops of Milford Haven.

SANDY HAVEN (17)

Sandy Haven beach is sand-wiched between the village of Sandy Haven and Herbrandston. Just below Herbrandston lies a sandy beach, which at low tide offers superb views of the estuary. Unsuitable for swimming however, because of unpredict-able estuary currents. Parking on both sides of the western and eastern sides of the estuary are limited.

LINDSWAY BAY (18)

Lindsway Bay is not suitable for bathing, but because of its position to the Milford Haven Waterway, it makes an ideal place for walking, bird watching and collecting shellfish. Enveloped by cliffs and large rocks, it also offers good views of St. Ann's Head from both the beach and the cliff top. South of the bay is Great Castle Head, the site of an Iron Age Fort. The beach is devoid of amenities and parking is a quarter of a mile away.

DALE (19)

If it's watersports you're interested in then this is the place to be. Dale is home to yachting, windsurfing and a watersports centre. It is also attractive to the sub-aqua
fraternity because of its wreck sites. Facilities in the attractive village overlooking the sea are good and there is a large carpark opposite the shingle beach.

WEST DALE (20)

West Dale is a stunning secluded cove, but its sand and shingle beach can be dangerous to swimmers because of undertows and unpredictable currents and hidden rocks. Access is via road or footpath through Dale, but parking is limited and there are no amenities.

Angle

Dale

MARLOES (21)

Marloes sands is a magnificent beach, characterised by outcrops of rocks and a large crescent of golden sand at low tide, which was inhabited from prehistoric to medieval times and which still bears the remains of 5th century huts. Another feature are the Three Chimneys - horizontal beds of rock, more than 400 million years old. The National Trust has a car park half a mile from the beach, but the nearest facilities are about a mile away in the village of Marloes.

MARTINS HAVEN (22)

Martins Haven is a small north facing cove with a pebble beach. Boat trips operate from here to the Skomer Nature Reserve. Facilities include toilets and parking.

MUSSELWICK (23)

Musselwick Sands is a fine sandy beach that is only exposed at low tide. Access is difficult and visitors need to be aware that the tide could cut them off. There are no amenities and parking at the start of the long footpath to the beach is limited.

ST. BRIDES HAVEN (24)

St. Bride's Haven is a sheltered cove with a beach of shingle, pebbles and rock pools, enhanced at low tide by sand. Interesting features near the beach include an early Christian Cemetery with stone lined graves and the remains of an old limekiln. There is limited parking near the church.

LITTLE HAVEN (25)

Little Haven is a small sandy cove with a slipway for small boats, including the local inshore rescue boat. There is a pay and display car park close to the beach and numerous facilities including pubs offering food and drink and other useful shops.

BROAD HAVEN WEST (26)

Broad Haven (west) is a large magnificent expanse of sand, which runs the entire length of Broad Haven village. It is a favourite with bathers and water-sport enthusiasts, and also has a great deal to interest geologists with an abundance of different rock formations. The village offers good facilities and a choice of car parks.

Little Haven

Broad Haven

Marloes

Broad Haven

Newgale

WEST COAST

DRUIDSTON HAVEN (27)

Druidston Haven, whilst being a long sandy beach, is not suitable for bathers because of strong currents. Enclosed on three sides by steep cliffs, access to the beach is by two footpaths. However, there is only limited parking on the roadside and there are no amenities.

NOLTON HAVEN (28)

Nolton Haven is a beach of sand and shingle with cliffs on either side. A red flag flying warns of danger to swimmers. There is a National Trust car park above the beach.

NEWGALE SANDS (29)

Newgale Sands is another broad expanse of sand exposed to the Atlantic gales, which acts as a magnet to surfers and other watersports enthusiasts. During summer lifeguards designate areas for swimmers and patrol this excellent beach. There is a shop, two cafes and a pub. Parking areas are good.

CAERBWDI BAY (30)

Caerbwdi Bay is a small sheltered beach of rock and pebble with sand visible at low tide. Close to St. Davids, it is reached along a half mile footpath leading from the A487 Solva to St. Davids road where there is limited parking. Although popular with walkers, the beach has no facilities.

CAERFAI BAY (31)

Caerfai Bay is the nearest beach to St. Davids and is popular with bathers, although at high tide the beach is covered leaving only rocks and boulders. A feature of the bay is the unusual purple sandstone along the cliffs, which was used to build St. Davids Cathedral. Parking is available above the beach, but there are no facilities.

WHITESANDS (32)

Whitesands, or to give is its Welsh name Traeth Mawr, is consistently rated one of Wales' very best seaside resorts. A large sandy beach in a magnificent setting,

Caerfai Bay

Newgale

Whitesands

Whitesands is well known for its views, glorious sunsets and crystal clear water. It is understandably popular with safe swimming and surfing areas designated by the lifeguards who patrol here during the summer months. If you can drag yourself away from the beach, there are some stunning walks with memorable views over the St. Davids Peninsula and Ramsey Island. Facilities at the beach are good and include a large car park. As an added bonus St. Davids, Britain's smallest city is close by with its many attractions and ancient cathedral.

PORTHMELGAN (33)

Porthmelgan is a sandy and secluded beach close to Whitesands. Access is along the coastal path from St. Davids or the car park at Whitesands.

ABEREIDDY BAY (34)

A few miles along the coast towards Fishguard will bring you to Abereiddy Bay which is vastly different to other beaches in the county in that it is covered in black sand. This is the result of waves constantly pounding the slate cliffs on either side.

Tiny fossil graptolites are found in pieces of shale, which have geological importance and should not be removed. Nearby is the Blue Lagoon, a flooded slate quarry, which serves as a reminder that the area was quarried until 1904 when the slate was shipped all around Britain. A large car park overlooks the beach but bathers should take care when going into the waters because of undercurrents.

TRAETH LLYFN (35)

Half a mile away from Abereiddy is Traeth Llyfn, a beautiful sandy beach whose only access is down steep steps. The beach is enclosed by cliffs and can be dangerous for swimming, especially in rough seas because of strong undertows. There is also the possibility of getting cut off by the incoming tide.

TREFIN (36)

Trefin is not suitable for bathing because of rocks and an unstable cliff, but there are excellent walks and views along the coast in both directions. Above the beach where parking is very limited, there are the remains of an old mill.

Abereiddy

Trefin

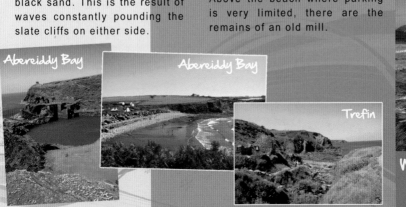

Abereiddy Bay

Abereiddy Bay

Trefin

Whitesands

ABERCASTLE (37)

Abercastle is an attractive sheltered harbour much favoured by fishermen, boat enthusiasts and walkers. Picturesque cottages overlook the shingle beach, which has a small car park. Above the beach to the right lies Carreg Samson, a 4,500 year old burial chamber.

ABERMAWR (38)

Abermawr is a large sheltered beach covered in pebbles, which is rarely visited by lots of people. Access is along a short path from the road where parking is limited and although there are no other amenities, the beach is well worth visiting. Like other Pembrokeshire beaches the low tide reveals the remains of a drowned forest.

PWLLGWAELOD (39)

Pwllgwaelod near Dinas Head is a small attractive sandy beach with views of Fishguard Bay and its harbour. It offers good cliff walking, a nature trail and the beach at Cwm-Yr-Eglwys.

CWM-YR-EGLWYS (40)

Overlooking the picturesque shingle and pebble beach are the remains of the 12th Century church of St. Brynach, which was destroyed during a fierce storm in 1859. The storm also wrecked over 100 ships. Access is along a narrow country lane off the main road between Fishguard and Cardigan, but is very much worth a visit. There is limited parking in a private car park.

NEWPORT PARROG (41)

The historic town of Newport stands near the mouth of the River Nevern where there are two beaches, one on either side of the estuary. The Parrog is on the southern side and although this is the more sheltered beach, unpredictable currents may make bathing dangerous. However the area is rich in prehistoric sites, including the Pentre Ifan burial chamber.

NEWPORT SANDS (42)

By far the more popular of Newport's two beaches, this vast expanse of sand on the northern side of the Nevern Estuary is backed by dunes and a golf course. A favourite spot for beach games and all manner of watersports, visitors should be careful of the dangerous currents around the mouth of the river. There's a car park above the beach and limited sand parking.

Newport Sands

Pwllgwaelod

Newport

Newport Parrog

Newport

Beach safety advice from the RNLI

WHEREVER POSSIBLE, SWIM AT A LIFEGUARDED BEACH

READ AND OBEY THE SAFETY SIGNS
USUALLY FOUND AT THE ENTRANCE TO THE BEACH

WHEN ON A LIFEGUARDED BEACH, FIND THE RED AND YELLOW
FLAGS AND ALWAYS SWIM OR BODYBOARD
BETWEEN THEM – THIS AREA IS PATROLLED BY LIFEGUARDS

NEVER SWIM ALONE

Red and yellow flags
Lifeguarded area: safest place to swim, bodyboard and use inflatables.

Black and white flags
For surfboards, kayaks and other non-powered craft. Never swim or bodyboard here.

Red flag
Danger! Never go in the water when the red flag is up, under any circumstances.

Orange windsock
Shows offshore winds or unsafe water conditions – never use an inflatable when the sock is flying.

IF YOU GET INTO TROUBLE STICK
YOUR HAND IN THE AIR
AND SHOUT FOR HELP

IF YOU SEE SOMEONE IN DIFFICULTY,
NEVER ATTEMPT A RESCUE. TELL A
LIFEGUARD, OR IF YOU CAN'T SEE A
LIFEGUARD, CALL 999 OR 112 AND ASK FOR THE COASTGUARD

FOR ALL IMPORTANT BEACH AND SAFETY INFORMATION VISIT:
www.rnli.org.uk

CEIBWR BAY (43)

Ceibwr Bay is an ideal base for coastal walks as the area boasts the highest cliffs in Pembrokeshire. The spectacular coastal scenery includes the Witches Cauldron (a cave, blowhole and natural arch) together with incredible folding of the cliff rock strata. Another attraction is the sight of Atlantic grey seals swimming offshore or basking on the rocks. Access to Ceibwr Bay is along a narrow road from the village of Moylegrove with limited parking above the bay.

POPPIT SANDS (44)

Situated at the mouth of the Teifi Estuary, Poppit Sands is a large expanse of sand which marks the northern border of Pembrokeshire and the northern end of the Pembrokeshire Coastal Path. The proximity of the beach to the town of Cardigan has made it very popular with visitors. Bathers should be aware of dangerous currents and heed the warning signs and lifeguard flags. The beach is backed by sand dunes and mudflats, both of which are sensitive, fragile environments important to wildlife, so should be avoided. Facilities close to the beach are good and include a large car park.

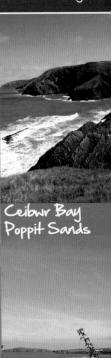

Ceibwr Bay
Poppit Sands

15

THE SOUTH COAST

There are four main holiday centres in South Pembrokeshire: Tenby, Saundersfoot, Pembroke and Narberth. Tenby and its near neighbour Saundersfoot are among Britain's favourite seaside resorts, while the ancient town of Pembroke, which celebrated 900 years of history in 1993, boasts one of Britain's best preserved medieval castles. Narberth too is an historic town with a Norman castle. All four centres are close to the countless visitor attractions and places of interest, and each provides an ideal base for exploring the glorious South Pembrokeshire coastline and countryside.

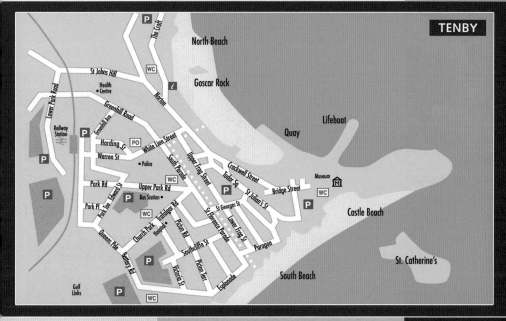

TENBY

DISTANCES: Fishguard 36m; Haverfordwest 19m; Milford Haven; 19m; Narberth 10m; Pembroke 10m; St. Davids 35m; Saundersfoot 3m; Carmarthen 27m; London 247m

Little has changed in Tenby since wealthy Victorians provided the finance to develop the town into one of Britain's most attractive holiday resorts. The Victorians came here for the good of their health, but it was the birth of the coming railway in 1866 which saw a ground swell of visitors. Were those early visitors to return today, they would no doubt be surprised to discover that Tenby is almost as they had left it and has seemingly escaped what many would regard as the "plague" of modern development. Much of the 13th century wall which surrounds Tenby is still intact and the narrow streets, freshly recobbled to imitate a bygone age are still packed tight with shops and places to eat. Although the bathing machines have long gone, the beaches have still retained their appeal. Both the North Beach and South Beach are a mecca for holidaymakers. The picturesque harbour too is unchanged except for the boats. In Victorian time Tenby's link with the sea was dominated by the boats of a once thriving fishing industry as opposed to the leisure craft.

Tenby

17

Tenby

THE SOUTH COAST
TENBY HARBOUR

Small, picturesque and brightly coloured by the neat painted cottages and spectrum of summer sail, Tenby harbour has a magnetic attraction. To sit on the harbour wall watching fishermen cast their lines and the boats sailing to and from Caldey Island is a pleasurable way of whiling away the time. Alternatively you can explore the lifeboat station passing Laston House on the way, where in the 19th century, Sir William Paxton played his part in helping to put Tenby on the map as a fashionable resort.

TUDOR MERCHANT'S HOUSE

Tenby's 15th century Tudor Merchant's House is the oldest furnished residence in the town. Standing on Quay Hill, between the harbour and Tudor square, its authentic furniture and fittings recreate the atmosphere of the period and illustrate the manner in which a successful Tudor merchant and his family would have lived. Three of the interior walls bear the remains of early Frescoes. Owned and managed by the National Trust, the house is open between March and October.

for further information call
01834 842279 or 01558 822800

TENBY LIFEBOAT STATION

Tenby is fortunate to have two lifeboats, the Hayden Miller and the smaller inshore rescue boat, the Georgina Stanley Taylor. The old lifeboat station, which is still standing, was established in 1852. The new lifeboat station is open to the public during the season for a fascinating insight into the workings of a modern lifeboat station. The new lifeboat, the Hayden Miller has been in operation since March 2006.

for further information go to
www.tenby rnli.co.uk

19

Giltar
HOTEL

Call today on 01834 842507

A warm welcome awaits you at one of Tenby's oldest yet most stylish hotels

An afternoon tea to remember, in our Victorian Tea lounge, a memory of days gone by

Scrumptious lunches and morning coffee await, or how about trying our regularly Sunday lunch menu - a restaurant with a stunning view

Catering for all your special occasions is our specialty - or join us for a Christmas party with a difference

Tribute nights and other special entertainment all through the year

Visit our website at www.giltar-hotel.co.uk
Tel. 01834 842507

TENBY MUSEUM AND ART GALLERY IS THE OLDEST INDEPENDENT MUSEUM IN WALES, HAVING BEEN ESTABLISHED IN 1878.

The museum has six main galleries – Geology and Archaeology; two art galleries, one showing works from the permanent collection including artists such as Gwen and Augustus John, David Jones, John Piper and Kyffin Williams whilst the second gallery houses frequently changing temporary exhibitions of work by artists associated with Pembrokeshire; the RNLI/maritime gallery; the Story of Tenby and a recreation of a Victorian/Edwardian shop. There are also smaller displays showing piracy and an antiquarian's study.

Tenby Museum and Art Gallery
Castle Hill
Tenby
Pembrokeshire
SA70 7BP
01834 842809
email: info@tenbymuseum.org.uk
web: www.tenbymuseum.org.uk

The museum has a shop and coffee shop with views over Carmarthen Bay; an audio tour; disabled access; research facilities, a Friends organisation and many activities for children.

TENBY MUSEUM AND GALLERY
Founded in 1878, Tenby Museum and Art Gallery is one of Tenby's main indoor attractions with the reputation of being one of the best local museums in the country. Situated on a spectacular site in part of the medieval castle, overlooking Castle Beach and Caldey Island. The galleries show the geology and archaeology of Pembrokeshire, its natural history, its bygones and the changing aspects of Tenby's developments up to the present day. The art gallery concentrates on artists with close local associations and works by others which portray Tenby and its locality. Augustus John was born in Tenby and his sister Gwen, now highly regarded, was brought up here, there is also a permanent exhibition of their works. Other artists represented

in the permanent collection include John Piper, David Jones, John Knapp-Fisher and Tenby born artist Nina Hamnett.

2011 exhibitions include: works from the museum's permanent collection; Jack Ashley; Geoff Yeomans; Cherry Pickles; Caro Flynn; Olivia Argent; Elisabeth Haines; Dennis Curry and Susan Sands.

Please see the website for further details:
www.tenbymuseum.org.uk

Tenby Museum and Art Gallery is open throughout the year. Full access for disabled visitors. Research facilities. Admission charges and concessions apply, whilst refreshments are available.

Tenby Museum

21

CALDEY ISLAND

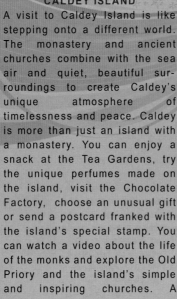

Caldey Monastery

A visit to Caldey Island is like stepping onto a different world. The monastery and ancient churches combine with the sea air and quiet, beautiful surroundings to create Caldey's unique atmosphere of timelessness and peace. Caldey is more than just an island with a monastery. You can enjoy a snack at the Tea Gardens, try the unique perfumes made on the island, visit the Chocolate Factory, choose an unusual gift or send a postcard franked with the island's special stamp. You can watch a video about the life of the monks and explore the Old Priory and the island's simple and inspiring churches. A walk up to the Lighthouse offers spectacular views of the Pembrokeshire coast and beyond. You can also follow the way-marked cliff and woodland paths, or simply relax on the sandy beach at Priory Bay. Caldey is a 20 minute boat trip from Tenby. Boats run every 20-30 minutes between 10am and 5pm from Easter to the end of October. Sailings are Monday to Saturday from May to September and Monday to Friday in April and October with selected Saturdays. A full range of products can be found at the Caldey Island shop, Quay Hill, Tenby.

Visit www.caldey-island.co.uk

NORMANDIE

BAR · ACCOMMODATION · RESTAURANT

The Normandie is a vibrant, colourful bar and restaurant with rooms, nestled between the Historic Town Walls and Upper Frog Street in the picturesque harbour town of Tenby, on the beautiful coast of West Wales.

Emphasis here is on great beers, good wines, delicious freshly made food and comfortable spacious ensuite bedrooms.

**The Normandie Upper Frog Street Tenby
Tenby Pembrokeshire West Wales
Tel: 01834 842227
Web: Normandietenby.co.uk
Email: info@Normandietenby.co.uk**

23

PENALLY

Nestling just west of Tenby is the pretty hillside village of Penally, which overlooks Tenby's golf course and South Beach. Penally is a well kept village complete with shop and pubs together with a good choice of accommodation including a first class hotel, the Penally Abbey, camping and caravan sites. A feature of the village is the 13th century church of St. Nicholas, which houses a memorial to the victims of the Tenby lifeboat who drowned when it capsized in 1834. Penally's proximity to Tenby, Lydstep, Manorbier, Freshwater East and Pembroke makes it an ideal holiday spot.

RITEC VALLEY QUAD BIKES, PENALLY

Ritec Valley Quad Bikes offers the ultimate in Quad bike entertainment whatever the weather, all year round.

Trail Riding is our serious activity (Minimum age 16) and needs to be booked in advance. We use 250cc semi-automatic sports quads (You need to be able to use gears).

We have over 12km of groomed routes to test every ability.

Arrive and Drive is for all ages and is carried out on Automatic quads (Minimum age 6). Arrive and Drive is for everyone under 16, families wishing to ride together or for seasoned quad bike addicts looking for a quick fix. No need to book, just Arrive and Drive.

We are open ALL YEAR but have a limited opening profile during the winter months.

For full info, please phone 01834 843390, or check out our website at: www.ritec-valley.co.uk Or email us on: thequadfather@btconnect.com

Visit Celtic Haven resort for
a great day out
away from the crowds...

Celtic HAVEN

Celtic Haven welcomes day visitors to enjoy this luxury resort on the cliff-top above Lydstep beach...

eat...

A stunning Italian influenced cliff-top restaurant with imaginative menus including pizza and pasta. Open daily for lunch including Lazy Sunday lunch. Evening openings vary with the season.
Bookings on 01834 870085

OPEN TO DAY VISITORS

play...

A Leisure Club that offers so much more - indoor pool and bubble room hot-tub, fitness suite, 9 hole golf course, indoor golf, tennis, jogging/walking mile, junior football pitch and children's adventure playground.
Bookings on 01834 870000

rest...

West Wales' only Elemis Premier Spa offering over 80 treatments including massages, facials, body wraps, manicures, pedicures and spray tans as well as luxury Spa rituals and breaks.
Bookings on 01834 871850

stay...

Luxury self-catering holidays in 12th Century cliff-top cottages for 2 - 12, overlooking Caldey Island. Free use of all the leisure facilities. Right on the coastal path.
Bookings on 01834 870000

Find us in the centre of Lydstep Village on the A4139 Tenby to Manorbier road
Celtic Haven, Lydstep, Tenby, Pembrokeshire SA70 7SG
Tel: 01834 870000   **www.celtichaven.co.uk**

ST FLORENCE

Once a medieval harbour standing on an inlet to the sea, St. Florence is a picturesque village of great charm and pretty cottages and boasts a past winner of the national "Wales in Bloom" competition. Here you will discover one of the area's last surviving areas's last surviving curious round chimneys, which are often described as Flemish in style. Also of interest is the 13th century parish church, featuring a Norman tower.

St. Florence

SAUNDERSFOOT

This bustling village is about three miles from Tenby, lying at the foot of a picturesque wooded valley. With its attractive harbour and extensive sandy beaches, it has established itself as a popular centre for sailing, fishing, watersports and traditional seaside holidays. Originally a small fishing village and home to two shipyards by the 1800's, Saundersfoot was suddenly caught up in the excitement of the black gold rush when high quality anthracite was discovered locally. Such was the demand for this coal that in 1829 the harbour was built, connected by rail to six mines. The railway ran along what is now The Strand and the coal was exported worldwide. It was not until the Second World War that coal shipments ceased, but by this time another flourishing industry was putting the village on the map - tourism. The rest they say is history.

Saundersfoot

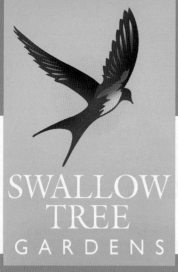

Swallow Tree Gardens
Saundersfoot
Pembrokeshire
SA69 9DE
Tel: 01834 812398
www.swallowtree.com
info@swallowtree.com

- Beautiful family-run Park with direct beach access.

- Luxury Pine Lodges with delightful seaviews. Spacious caravans.

- Superb Leisure Facility with large, indoor heated pool, sauna and steamroom. Open to Day Visitors.

- Revive Spa offers relaxing Elemis treatments, Organics Spray tan, Jessica, Minx Nails and much more......Open to Day Visitors.

- Free wifi

AMROTH AND PENDINE

The small coastal village of Amroth is just seven miles from Tenby and four miles from Saundersfoot. It is a wild and beautifully unspoiled location. In summer the wonderful expanse of gently shelving sand, exposed at low tide, makes it a favourite beach for families and anglers alike. The village, spread along the narrow seafront, has plenty of good facilities, including restaurants, pubs, gift shops, caravan parks and holiday homes. Attractions close by include Colby Woodland Garden, which is owned by the National Trust, and Pendine Sands, a resort made famous in the 1920's by speed king Sir Malcolm Campbell. In April 1926, Parry Thomas set a new World Land Speed record of 171.02mph driving his car "Babs". The following year he died at the wheel of "Babs" while attempting to regain the record. The car was buried in the sand by local villagers with the consent of his family and was recovered for restoration in March 1969.

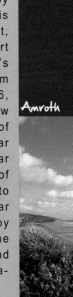

Amroth

THE SOUTH COAST

MARROS RIDING CENTRE

Located on the coast road between Amroth and Pendine we offer horse riding for everyone (weight limit applies). Combination sessions great chance to learn some new skills before trekking in the woods. Treks of varying lengths are offered. Beach rides are for experienced riders over 16 years of age. Own-a-pony Days are offered to children over 8 years and includes a riding lesson, trek and looking after their pony needs. For our younger riders (2 – 4 years) we offer short pony rides.

We really love what we do and know you will have an experience to remember when you ride with us. See you soon.

All enquiries 01994 453777 speak to our friendly, experienced staff who will be happy to discuss your requirements and book you in. A warm welcome awaits you.

WISEMAN'S BRIDGE

A tiny hamlet, best known for its inn and rocky beaches, nestles on the coast between Saundersfoot and Amroth and at low tide it is possible to walk across the sands to either. You can also walk to Saundersfoot through the tunnels that once formed part of the all important railway link between local mines and Saundersfoot harbour.

KILGETTY

Before the bypass was built, the main road into South Pembrokeshire from the east went through Kilgetty village. However, the place remains an important centre for visitors, with its, railway station, and shops, it's also close to several major attractions. The neighbouring village of Begelly is well known for Folly Farm and is a short distance west of Kilgetty as are the villages of Broadmoor and East Williamston, where there are first class caravan parks and a pub.

STEPASIDE

It is hard to believe now but in the 19th century this quiet little hamlet was a hive of industrial activity after the Pembrokeshire Iron and Coal Company built the Kilgetty Ironworks here in 1848. Iron ore, in plentiful supply from seams along the cliffs between Amroth and Saundersfoot, was smelted in the blast furnace using locally produced limestone and coal and the iron transported to Saundersfoot harbour by railway.

COLBY WOODLAND GARDEN

Described by the National Trust as one of their most beautiful properties in Pembrokeshire, the garden is part of the Colby Estate, which was established by John Colby, the 19th century mining entrepreneur. The garden is a spectacular blaze of colour from early spring to the end of June. On site is a National Trust shop where refreshments are available, along with a gallery, plant sales, toilets and a car park.

for more information
01834 811885

Wiseman's
Bridge

Wiseman's
Bridge

Colby

Colby

PEMBROKE DOCK
LONDON ROAD
TELEPHONE: 01646 687962
6am until 11pm SEVEN DAYS A WEEK

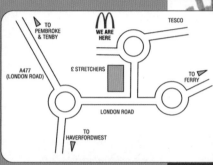

HAVERFORDWEST
CARADOCS WELL ROAD,
MERLINS BRIDGE
TELEPHONE: 01437 769513
Sunday to Thursday 5am to 11pm
Friday and Saturday 5am to 2am*

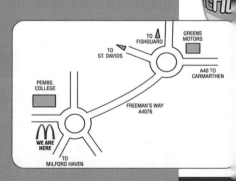

*Drive Thru only after 11pr

MANORBIER CASTLE

Families love to explore Manorbier Castle and bring a little bit of history to life.

Opening times: Daily from 6th April to 30th September 2011 10.00am to 6.00pm. Every weekend in October and half term.

Admission: £4.00 adults, £1.50 children, £3.00 senior citizens

Excellent local transport: Bus no. 349 Tenby-Haverfordwest stops at the gate. Train station 3/4 mile away.

Dogs admitted on a lead • Convenient parking • Toilets • Gift Shop Quality coffee and tasty light bites • Castle Tel: 01834 871394

www.manorbiercastle.co.uk

Manorbier

MANORBIER

Manorbier is a small seaside village midway between Tenby and Pembroke, and is best known for two striking features, the beach and a well preserved medieval castle. The castle, which enjoys a spectacular location overlooking the bay, was the birthplace of Gerald of Wales, a much respected medieval writer and a man of many talents whose two major works are still in print today. But Gerald wasn't the only one to find inspiration in Manorbier, George Bernard Shaw spent several months there, and prior to her marriage in 1912 Virginia Woolf was a regular summer visitor.

THE BIER HOUSE

The Bier House in the centre of the village was built in 1900 to house the parish bier, a funeral hand cart that was used to carry the dead to the burial ground. Now the building has been restored and provides an information point relating to the history of the parish.

Open All Day throughout the year.
Food is served every lunch time and every evening throughout the year

The Carew Inn, Carew, Tenby, SA70 8SL
Tel: (01646) 651267   www.carewinn.co.uk

| TRADITIONAL DINING | FRIENDLY BAR & LOUNGE | MARQUEE FOR DINING & EATING | CHILDREN'S PLAY AREA | OUTDOOR BAR B Q AREA |

We are open from 11am to 11pm everyday (except Christmas Day).

Food is served 12 noon to 2:30pm and 6pm to 9pm. Monday to Saturday.

On Sundays we offer a delicious Sunday Lunch from 12 noon to 5pm, and then our normal menu from 6pm to 9pm

We have two rooms that will accommodate parties of up to 36 for meals, a comfortable lounge bar and an atmospheric public bar.

Real Fires, Real Ales and a Real Welcome

Tudor Lodge Restaurant, Pembroke Road, Jameston, SA70 7SS
Telephone 01834 871212   www.tudorlodgejameston.co.uk

LAMPHEY

The village of Lamphey is the site of what is left of the Bishop's Palace, built in the 13th century by the Bishops of St. Davids and now in the care of Cadw who are responsible for Welsh Historic Monuments. The centuries old ruins are an evocative reminder of the great power enjoyed by the medieval Bishops of St. Davids. The comfortable palace buildings were set among well stocked fishponds, plump orchards and an extensive vegetable garden. In its heyday Lamphey boasted an impressive 144 acre park, a deer herd, windmill, two watermills and a dovecote. The palace's finest architectural features include the great hall built by Bishop Henry de Gower in the 14th century and the 16th century chapel.

for opening times and admission prices ring the Pembroke Library & Information Centre on 01437 776499 or CADW (Welsh Historic Monuments) on 01443 336000

Lamphey Palace

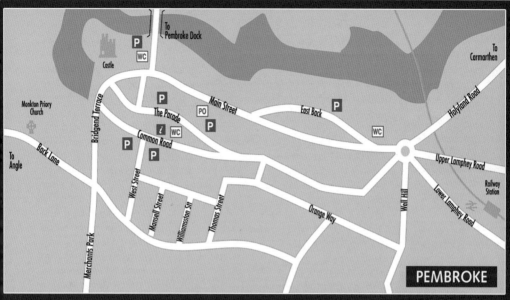

PEMBROKE

PEMBROKE

DISTANCES: Fishguard 26m, Haverfordwest 10m, Milford Haven 5m, Narberth 15m St. Davids 26m, Tenby 12m, Carmarthen 32m, London 252m.

Pembroke is a small but charming walled town with a genteel atmosphere, a 900 year old history and much to recommend it to visitors. Like many other Welsh towns, Pembroke grew up around its medieval castle. This magnificent structure, the birthplace of Henry VII enjoys a spectacular location offering breathtaking views from the top of its famous keep. The castle is in a very good state of repair having undergone an extensive restoration programme that started as far back as 1928. Throughout the year the castle is the venue for many important events, several of which are traditions rooted firmly in the towns medieval past. The castle also plays host to such attractions including Shakespearean productions, medieval banquets, military tattoos and displays by the Sealed Knot Society. The Norman Conquest saw Pembroke develop into the main base from which the invaders increased their stranglehold on West Wales. The town became a major market centre with regular fairs. Now every October this tradition is still remembered when the town celebrates the Pembroke Fair which attracts visitors from far and wide.

THE SOUTH COAST

THE COURTYARD DELI CAFE

In what was believed to once have been a stable, is now home to The Courtyard Deli. After several months of nurturing from what was merely a shell, the Courtyard Deli was opened. Tucked away behind Pembroke main street, and at the rear of the natwest bank the Courtyard Deli offers a large selection of freshly made home cooked foods, all made to order. There is plenty of seating within the Courtyard Deli from downstairs to upstairs and then to outside. Our Aim when launching the Courtyard Deli was that we would create a warm friendly atmosphere, time for a chat or being able to pop in on your own and just watch the world go by.

Our passion for Pembrokeshire is at the heart of what we produce and this has been reflected by the support we have received enabling us to go from strength to strength.

So, when in Pembroke, why not call in, and relax in the "cwtch", or sit outside and watch the world go by by enjoying a coffee with a slice of homemade Bara Brith or Welsh Cakes, maybe the homemade quiche with salad garnish and Mediterranean bread, or enjoy one of Cynthia's Famous Meringues, with local staff happy to help with any information that you may need.

for further information
ring 01646 622144

One of the town's attractions is Mill Pond, formed by one of two tidal creeks. It's a popular beauty spot with visitors and locals alike because of the wildlife it attracts. Swans, herons, cormorants and if you are lucky enough even otters can be seen along this peaceful stretch of water. As visitors can explore Pembroke, they will see evidence of the town's ancient and extensive walls, which are a throwback to the 13th century, when the townsfolk demanded that stone walls be built to protect their cottages from raiders. Under Norman rule, it established itself as an important trading port and hit a peak between the 17th and 19th centuries. In 1977, Pembroke was designated an outstanding Conservation Area.

Pembroke Castle

39

Pembroke Festival

THE SOUTH COAST

EDU TOYS @
PEMBROKE POST OFFICE

Having recently completed a major refurbishment, Edu Toys @ Pembroke Post Office has now doubled it's retail space allowing a wider range of childrenswear, gifts and educational toys. A number of new ranges are now available including a beautiful selection of children's jewellery – a perfect christening or birthday gift. Wooden and educational toys are a must for any child, and we continually add new products to our range. Children learn so much through play and this is our emphasis when considering new toys. If it is something different you are looking for, why not pay us a visit.

tel: 01646 682737

PEMBROKE VISITOR
CENTRE

Built in 1993 to coincide with the town's 900th birthday celebrations, this is an integral part of Pembroke's superb new Tourist Information Centre. Displays and exhibits tell the story of Pembroke and there is a choice of books, maps and souvenirs on sale.

tel: 01437 776499

PEMBROKE CASTLE

Pembroke Castle is one of the best preserved medieval castles in Wales. Open to visitors all year round, it is an intriguing place to explore. The wide walls are honeycombed with a seemingly endless system of rooms, passageways and spiralling flights of narrow stone steps; interpretive displays and informative panels give a fascinating insight into the castles origins and long history. One of the most impressive features is the distinctive round keep, which was built soon after 1200. It is 75ft high and the views from the top in all directions are nothing short of magnificent. From this lofty position it is easy to understand why the Normans were well aware that the site was ideal for fortification, a low rocky peninsula between two tidal creeks offering superb natural defences. They quickly established a wooden fortress and in 1200 work began on the castle itself. Harri Tudor (Henry VII) was born in Pembroke Castle on 28th January 1457 of an Anglesey family. In 1485 he returned from exile in France, landing at Millbay on the Milford Haven waterway. From there he marched a growing army of largely untrained volunteers across country to Bosworth Field in Leicestershire to confront Richard III. Against the odds, Henry's forces defeated Richard and Henry became King of England. So ended the War of the Roses and began the Tudor dynasty.

Tel: 01646 681510 or 684585

41

PEMBROKE DOCK

In the early 19th century it was nothing more than a small coastal village known as Paterchurch. But when in 1814 the lease expired on the Royal Naval Dockyard in Milford Haven, the Admiralty decided to move its shipbuilding operation across the water and further from the mouth of the estuary and Paterchurch was designated the ideal site. Hence began an amazing transformation, which saw naval architects lay out the distinctive grid pattern of wide streets so characteristic of today's Pembroke Dock. In 1930 a major part of the dockyard site was transferred from the Admiralty to the Air Ministry, and in the following year the Royal Air Force established a seaplane base, operated by Southampton flying boats of 210 Squadron.

Pembroke Dock

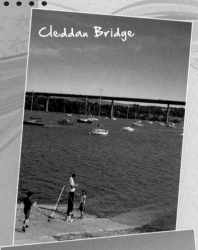

Cleddau Bridge

Gun Tower Museum

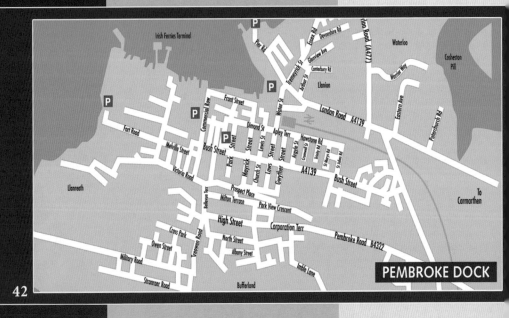

PEMBROKE DOCK

Cleddau Bridge

Gun Tower Museum

1938 saw the arrival of the first Sunderland flying boat, the aircraft with which Pembroke Dock is most associated. During the Second World War the Sunderlands gave sterling service and eventually stayed on here until 1957. In March 1993, during one of the lowest tides of the century, three men discovered the remains of a rear gun turret and fairing, part of a Sunderland flying boat of 201 Squadron that crashed in the Haven Waterway during a training exercise in March 1954. Today Pembroke Dock is better known as a ferry port with excellent boating and watersport facilities.

43

THE SOUTH COAST

THE GUN TOWER MUSEUM

The Gun Tower formed part of the fortifications of the Milford Haven waterway. The tower's specific role was to help defend and protect the Royal Naval Dockyard, though in the event the only threat came from the air raids in the Second World War, long after the dockyard had closed. Built in 1851 to repel "unwelcome guests", the imposing dressed stone tower now welcomes visitors with open arms. Visitors are offered an intriguing experience of the life lived by Queen Victoria's soldiers and marines, who waited, in these cramped quarters, for the French invasion that never came. Three floors of colourful models, pictures and full scale displays include life sized soldiers and many authentic relics. A splendid panoramic model shows us the town's Royal Dockyard. Here 250 warships were built, along with five elegant Royal yachts. During World War Two, Pembroke Dock was the world's largest operational flying boat base. Important features include an original working roof cannon and the basement magazine, where 20,000 lbs of gunpowder were stored, plus an educational video.

for all information
call: 01646 622246

Green Bridge of Wales

Stack Rocks

THE CASTLEMARTIN PENINSULA

The Castlemartin Peninsula, which is also known as the Angle Peninsula, typifies the unique appeal of South Pembrokeshire in that it has many special features of interest to many different groups. Birdwatchers flock here for the colonies of guillemots, razorbills, kittiwakes, choughs and other species that nest along the cliffs and rock formations. There are outstanding examples of fissures, sea caves, blowholes, natural arches and stacks, the result of continual sea erosion of the carboniferous limestone cliffs. Anthropologists have been excited by the discovery of bones and implements in caves which 20,000 years ago gave shelter to the region's earliest known human inhabitants. Historians are enchanted by such mysteries as tiny St. Govan's Chapel and by the remains of Iron Age Forts and other ancient sites. For visitors who are here to simply enjoy a holiday, there are attractions such as the Bosherston Lily Ponds and the superb beaches of Barafundle, Broad Haven, Freshwater West and West Angle Bay to savour. The peninsula is also well known for its 6000 acre Ministry of Defence tank range. This means that a large section of the coastline is inaccessible, one of the very few places in Pembrokeshire that the coast path is diverted inland.

FRESHWATER EAST

From the small coastal village of Freshwater East, visitors are ideally placed to explore the stunning coastline. Freshwater East is a popular resort in its own right. The Trewent Park holiday complex provides self-catering accommodation close to the beach and there is a touring caravan park.

STACKPOLE

Stackpole has its name in Norse origins, and the village as it stands today is in a different place from its original medieval site, The centre of the old village is about half a mile to the southwest, marked by the remains of a preaching cross.

STACKPOLE QUAY

The National Trust owns and manages Stackpole Quay, which it acquired in 1976 as part of the 2000 acres of Stackpole Estate. This acquisition also included the stretch of coastline between here and Broad Haven, under the Enterprise Neptune initiative, a scheme launched in 1965 to save and protect Britain's precious and threatened coastline. Stackpole Quay was originally a private quay built for the estate, so that coal could be imported and limestone shipped out from the quarry. It is claimed that this is Britain's smallest harbour, however pleasure boats are now the only craft that use the stone jetty.

Stackpole Quay

Freshwater East

45

STACKPOLE QUARRY

As part of its management of the Stackpole Estate, the National Trust has utilised the natural geological features of the old quarry near Stackpole Quay to create an area in which visitors, including those with special needs, can enjoy countryside recreation. Around the top of the quarry is a circular path giving spectacular vistas of the surrounding landscape and coastline. Down below, on the quarry floor, are sheltered picnic and barbecue areas and an archery bay. In addition, the cleared rock faces a present a challenge to experienced climbers and abseilers. Everyone can use the quarry's facilities, but groups or event organisers should first contact the warden. Close to the quarry is the main car park for Stackpole Quay, along with the National Trust holiday cottages, carefully converted from old buildings.

for more information about holiday letting call 0870 458411 or visit www.nationaltrust.org.uk for details of the quarry facilities call 01646 661359

BOSHERSTON

For such a small village, Bosherston certainly enjoys its fair share of fame due to its proximity to several major tourist attractions in South Pembrokeshire. These include the delightful Bosherston Lily Ponds, part of the Stackpole Lakes, and Broad Haven beach. On days when the M.O.D tank range is not in use and the access roads are open, Bosherston is also the gateway to the remarkable St. Govan's Chapel and some of the best limestone cliff scenery in Europe, with coastal features such as St. Govan's Head, Huntsman's Leap, Stack Rocks and the Green Bridge of Wales.

Bosherston

Lily Ponds

The village is also home to the 14th century St.Michael's Church which has an unusual cross of the same period standing in the churchyard. Much older still is a huge boulder, originating from Scotland, which was deposited at Bosherston by a moving glacier during the last Ice Age. Bosherston also has ample parking, with alternative parking above Broad Haven, and a pub, tearooms and toilets. When the tank range access road is open there is also plenty of free parking at St. Govan's.

to find out range road access times ask at any Tourist Information Centres or ring Merrion Camp on 01646 662287 or Bosherston Tearooms on 01646 661216.

BOSHERSTON LILY PONDS AND BROAD HAVEN

When the Campbells of Stackpole created the lakes and lily ponds to enhance their estate in the late 18th and early 19th centuries, they were unwittingly setting the scene for an attraction that brings thousands of annual visitors to the small village of Bosherston. Covering more than 80 acres, the lakes and lily ponds are the largest area of fresh water in the Pembrokeshire Coast National Park and are part of the Stackpole National Nature Reserve. They are usually at their very best around June, when the lilies are in full bloom, but even in winter they provide easy and fascinating walks. They also offer good coarse fishing and are well stocked with roach, pike, tench and eels. Fishing permits are available from the tearooms in the village. There are in fact three lakes, artificially created by the deliberate flooding of narrow limestone valleys. The lily ponds occupy only the western lake, which is fed by underwater springs. Grey herons are regular visitors, and the total lakes area attracts a great variety of birds and wildlife, including coots, moorhens, mallard, teal, swans, cormorants, kingfishers, buzzards and many smaller winged visitors such as blue damseflies and emperor dragonflies. Over 20 species of duck alone have been recorded here.

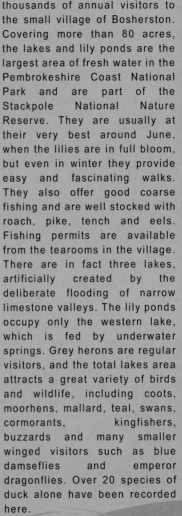

Lilies in bloom

Broad Haven

Vi's Tearooms

Broad Haven

47

ST. GOVAN'S CHAPEL

Remarkable St. Govan's Chapel is one of the wonders of Pembrokeshire. A tiny building hidden in a fissure in the cliff near St. Govan's car park, the restored chapel nestles at the bottom of a flight of narrow steps. It is said that if you count the steps on the way down and then count them on the way back up, the numbers won't tally. Though it occupies the site of a 5th century hermit's cell, the age of the chapel itself is not known for sure; expert estimates put it at no older than 11th century. St. Govan is reputedly buried beneath the altar. It is also said that Sir Gawaine, one of King Arthur's Knights, lived here in isolation. Yet another legend tells of the holy well's miraculous healing powers. St. Govan's Chapel is close to St. Govan's Head, the most southerly point in Pembrokeshire and is well worth seeing for its dramatic cliff scenery.

St Govans Head

gaping chasm in the cliffs west of St. Govan's Chapel. On looking back he was so horrified by the prospect of what might have happened that the shock killed him anyway.

GREEN BRIDGE OF WALES

Standing just 150 yards or so from Stack Rocks car park, the Green Bridge of Wales is an excellent example of a natural limestone arch. It was formed by the joining of two caves, each created by erosion of the rock by constant bombardment by the sea, and eventually the roof of the arch will collapse and leave a pinnacle of rock, a stack standing in the sea. This is the same process that created Stack Rocks. The Green Bridge of Wales is easy to see and photograph in full profile with complete safety thanks to the wooden viewing platform constructed especially for the purpose by the National Park Authority.

HUNTSMAN'S LEAP

According to legend, a horseman fleeing from pursuers miraculously leaped across this

Green Bridge

St Govans Chapel

Stack Rocks

St Govans Head

PEMBROKESHIRE WHERE TO EAT GUIDE

Restaurant Key

(10) MAP REF FOUND ON PAGE 3

PEMBROKESHIRE PRODUCE ACCREDITED

LICENSED

FAMILY FRIENDLY

P PARKING

DISABLED FRIENDLY

---

1 MAP PG 3

THE GILTAR HOTEL

9 ESPLANADE, TENBY, SA70 7DU, Tel: 01834 842507
www.giltar-hotel.co.uk

Come and relax in our beautiful restaurant overlooking the sea towards Caldey. We are open for lunches and dinner in the evening, as well as the traditional Sunday Lunch.

SEE ADVERT PAGE 20

---

1 MAP PG 3

CHINA TOWN CHINESE RESTAURANT

TEMPLE HOUSE, LOWER FROG STREET, TENBY, SA70 7HZ
Tel: 01834 843557

Fully Licensed Chinese and Cantonese Restaurant including takeaway with up to 20% discount off the restaurant menu. Telephone orders and bookings welcome.
Our Special Takeaway Set Lunch Menu offers Great Value for Money on Light Bite and Happy Lunch Box to suit everyone's appetite and pocket.

---

1 MAP PG 3

THE NORMANDIE

UPPER FROG ST, TENBY, SA70 7JD,
Tel: 01834 842227
www.normandietenby.co.uk

A vibrant, colourful bar and restaurant with rooms nestled between the Historic Town Walls and Upper Frog Street. Emphasis is on great food, wines and beers and excellent accommodation.

SEE ADVERT PAGE 23

MAP PG 3 | ## FIVE ARCHES TAVERN & RESTAURANT

ST GEORGE'S ST, TENBY, SA70 7JB, Tel: 01834 842513

A highly recommended venue with a warm welcome serving a variety of homemade dishes on the menu.

SEE ADVERT PAGE 18

 MAP PG 3 | **D. FECCIS & SONS FISH AND CHIP RESTAURANT & TAKEAWAY**

OXFORD HOUSE, LOWER FROG ST, TENBY, SA70 7HS
Tel: 01834 842484

Established in 1935, our Converted Coach Inn house has grown into one of Britain's finest Fish and Chip restaurants and take away. Offering a wide range of quality fish & chips and other chip shop favourites all cooked to order.
Coeliac batter available.

SEE ADVERT PAGE 19

FISH & CHIP
QUALITY AWARD
Valid to February
2013
qualityfishandchips.co.uk

 MAP PG 3 | ## PENALLY ABBEY

PENALLY, NR TENBY, SA70 7PY, Tel: 01834 843033
www.penally-abbey.com

Delicious, unpretentious food in beautiful surroundings.

SEE ADVERT INSIDE COVER

 MAP PG 3 | ## Waves bar & restaurant

CELTIC HAVEN, LYDSTEP, TENBY, SA70 7SG, Tel: 01834 870085
www.celtichaven.co.uk/restaurants

WAVES Italian influenced bar & restaurant. With a stunning view and a fabulous Italian influenced menu Waves is the perfect place for a relaxing dinner, either in the tastefully decorated dining-room or on the sunny terrace. Whether you choose pizza, pasta or specialty meat & fish dishes from the different regions of Italy, dining at Waves is sure to be an enjoyable experience.

WAVES
the Italian influence

SEE ADVERT PAGE 26

50

THE LYDSTEP TAVERN

MAP PG 3 3

LYDSTEP, TENBY, SA70 7SG, Tel: 01834 871521

Good food and fine ale in a
traditional country inn.

**SEE ADVERT
PAGE 34**

SWALLOW TREE GARDENS

MAP PG 3 50

**SWALLOW TREE GARDENS, SAUNDERSFOOT, SA69 9DE
Tel: 01834 812398, www.swallowtree.com**

* Excellent Food
* Delightful Sea Views
* Fresh Fish Specials
* Families Welcome

SEE ADVERT PAGE 28

A TASTE OF CORNWALL

MAP PG 3 50

**CAMBRIAN TERRACE, SAUNDERSFOOT, PEMBS, SA69 9ER
Tel: 07800728060**

A large & varied menu of freshly baked pasties including many
vegetarian options. Freshly prepared
baguettes and paninis with hot or
cold fillings. Eat in or take-away.

SEE ADVERT PAGE 29

WISEMAN'S BRIDGE INN

MAP PG 3 19

**WISEMAN'S BRIDGE, SAUNDERSFOOT, SA69 9AU
Tel: 01834 813236, www.wisemansbridgeinn.co.uk**

The setting for this traditional pub couldn't be better. Enjoy a meal
or even just a quiet drink whilst taking in the superb sweeping
views of Carmarthen Bay, either from our dining room or from our
garden that extends right down to the beach. A range of real ales
is on offer, together with a bar
snack and evening meals menu.

MAP PG 3

HASTY BITE (PEMBROKE DOCK)

UNIT 35 - 36, DIMOND STREET, PEMBROKE DOCK , SA72 6JA
Tel: 01646 682856

A small family style business offering a friendly atmosphere with Quality food at reasonable prices. We are able to provide hot and cold food to eat in or take away. We also are able to cater for buffets big or small upon request.

SEE ADVERT PAGE 43

 MAP PG 3

THE CLEDDAU BRIDGE HOTEL

ESSEX ROAD, PEMBROKE DOCK, SA72 6EG, Tel: 01646 685961
www.cleddauhotel.co.uk

Excellent a la carte restaurant serving high quality locally sourced fare, combining a superb menu with fantastic waterway views.

SEE ADVERT
INSIDE REAR
COVER

 MAP PG 3

THE COURTYARD DELI CAFE

Tel: 01646 622144
Email: thecourtyarddelicafe@yahoo.co.uk

Homecooked food * Family Run Business * Outside catering
Special dietery requirements catered for
Friendly homely welcome

SEE ADVERT
PAGE 38

 MAP PG 3

MCDONALDS

LONDON ROAD, PEMBROKE DOCK, SA72 6BP
Tel: 01646 687962

Excellent quality food for the family in a hurry.
Recently refurbished restaurant and with
drive thru facility.

SEE ADVERT
PAGE 32

THE CAREW INN

MAP PG 3 40

THE CAREW INN, CAREW, TENBY, SA70 8SL
Tel: (01646) 651267   www.carewinn.co.uk

Open All Day throughout the year. Food is
served every lunch time and every evening
throughout the year

SEE ADVERT PAGE 35

THE TUDOR LODGE

MAP PG 3 49

TUDOR LODGE RESTAURANT, PEMBROKE ROAD,
JAMESTON, SA70 7SS
Tel:01834 871212 www.tudorlodgejameston.co.uk

We are open from 11am to 11pm everyday
(except Christmas Day).
Real Fires, Real Ales and a Real Welcome

SEE ADVERT PAGE 35

HASTY BITE (HAVERFORDWEST)

MAP PG 3 9

24, HIGH ST, (under The Pink Cat Shop) HAVERFORDWEST, SA61 2DA,
Tel: 01437 783842

A small family style business offering a friendly atmosphere with Quality food at
reasonable prices. We are able to provide hot and cold food to eat in or take
away. We also are able to cater for buffets big or small upon request.

SEE ADVERT PAGE 71

MCDONALDS

MAP PG 3 9

CARADOCS WELL ROAD,HAVERFORDWEST, SA61 1XJ
Tel: 01437 769513

Excellent quality food for the
family in a hurry. Recently refurbished
restaurant and with drive thru facility.

SEE ADVERT PAGE 32

MAP PG 3

THE REFECTORY AT ST DAVIDS CATHEDRAL

ST DAVIDS CATHEDRAL, THE CLOSE, ST DAVIDS, SA62 6PE
Tel: 01437 721760 www.stdavidscathedral.org.uk

We serve delicious food and drink in one of the most beautiful spaces in Wales. Our lunch menu changes daily and we always have freshly made sandwiches and cakes on offer, plus excellent tea and coffee.
We are also a licensed premises.

SEE ADVERT PAGE 116

THE REFECTORY at ST DAVIDS

MAP PG 3

THE BISHOPS

CROSS SQUARE, ST DAVIDS, SA62 6SL Tel: 01437 720422

A family freehouse with a varied menu.
Meals available 12pm to 2.30pm & 6pm to 9.30pm. With a large terraced garden, ample indoor seating and close to the Cathedral.
Open April to September.

SEE ADVERT PAGE 115

12 MAP PG 3

THE SLOOP INN

PORTHGAIN, SA62 5BN Tel: 01348 831449

The Sloop Inn, probably the best known pub in the county, is situated just 100 yards from the harbour of Porthgain. The menu is varied, catering for all tastes including vegetarians and children.
A full menu is available 12.00 - 2.30 & 6.00 - 9.30 every day including specials, Sunday Lunches, plus limited choice in the afternoon high season.

SEE ADVERT PAGE 123

24 MAP PG 3

CWM DERI VINEYARD AND ESTATE

MARTLETWY, SA67 8AP, Tel: 01834 891274

Whether it is a simple cup of coffee and cake, a cream tea or a full meal, the restaurant and cafe at Cwm Deri can satisfy your needs. Using only the finest ingredients from Pembrokeshire wherever possible. Our chef Daniel can cater the food requirements of individuals or for parties of up to forty or more. Enjoy a tasting of our wines and liqueurs, either in our shop or on our patio and terrace, with a commanding view over the vineyard.

SEE ADVERT PAGE 174

Cwm Deri
Vineyard
and ESTATE

MAP PG 3

FIRE & ICE

66 ST JAMES STREET, NARBERTH, SA67 7DB

A selection of locally produced ice creams in 12 fantastic flavours. Dairy free Sorbets, Sugar free & Gluten free available. Take Home Tubs available (0.75ltr & 1ltr) flavours change weekly.

SEE ADVERT PAGE 155

 MAP PG 3 **LLYS-Y-FRAN RESERVOIR RESTAURANT & TEAROOMS**

CLARBESTON ROAD, HAVERFORDWEST, SA63 4RR, Tel: 01437 532694

With beautiful views and a sun patio that's open during the summer months. A function room is available for wedding receptions, private parties, seminars etc. please ring for further details

SEE ADVERT PAGE 149

 MAP PG 3 (NARBERTH) **THE CREATIVE CAFE** (HAVERFORDWEST) **MAP PG 3** 9

SPRING GARDENS, NARBERTH	22 HIGH ST, HAVERFORDWEST
PEMBROKESHIRE SA67 7BT	PEMBROKESHIRE SA61 2DA
Tel: 01834 861651	TEL: 01437 766698

The Creative Café is a paint-your-own pottery studio with a difference - where YOU can be the artist... whether you're artistic or not! Come and create your very own ceramic masterpiece in either of our two studios.

SEE ADVERT PAGE 157

NARBERTH ONLY

---

13 **MAP PG 3**

THE FARMERS ARMS

MATHRY, NR FISHGUARD, SA62 5HB
Tel: 01348 831284,
www.farmersarmsmathry.co.uk

Good food and fine ale in a traditional country inn.

SEE ADVERT PAGE 124

FRESHWATER EAST INN

FRESHWATER EAST, PEMBROKE, SA71 5LE
Tel: 01646-672828 email: enquiries@freshwaterinn.co.uk

Stunning views from the restaurant * Home cooked food to order
Licensed * Family friendly * Disabled access * Dog friendly

**SEE ADVERT
PAGE 45**

THE ROYAL OAK NEWPORT CURRY HOUSE

WEST STREET, NEWPORT, SA42 0TA, Tel: 01239 820632

Established as the "Curry House" of Newport, we also
specialise in fresh fish and grills, using local produce
wherever possible. Vegetarians & special diets are
catered for and traditional Sunday Lunch is served all
year round.

SEE ADVERT PAGE 134

QUAYSIDE TEAROOMS

LAWRENNY QUAY, LAWRENNY, SA68 0PR
Tel: 01646 651574

Fantastic innovative menu with a variety of dishes
made from fresh local produce, most notably local
crab and shellfish, with unparalleled
waterside views.

SEE ADVERT PAGE 172

CAFE TORCH (TORCH THEATRE

TORCH THEATRE, ST. PETER'S ROAD, MILFORD HAVEN, SA73 2BU
Web:www.torchtheatre.co.uk Tel: 01646 695267

Open daily for lunches, sandwiches, snacks and homemade cakes,
it's also a great meeting place. In our modern, comfy surroundings
you can enjoy a bit of peace and quiet, a great terrace to sit out on
when the weather is fine and WiFi access makes it suitable for a
quiet working lunch.

SEE ADVERT PAGE 83

PEMBROKESHIRE'S PREMIER ATTRACTIONS

Pembrokeshire is fortunate to have many top class attractions which will enhance any holiday whatever the weather. There are top family attractions such as Folly Farm, Oakwood Theme Park, The Dinosaur Park, Heatherton and Manor House Wildlife Park now owned by Anna Ryder Richardson. If the weather takes a turn for the worst then the new Blue Lagoon development at Bluestone offers the best in wet fun under a dry roof. Contained within this section is a guide to all of the best attractions that Pembrokeshire has to offer to suit all tastes and ages.

Anna Ryder-Richardson's
MANOR HOUSE
Wildlife Park

OPEN ALL YEAR
Open all year and with four Zoonique Walkthroughs this Wonderful Wildlife Park offers 52 acres of organically packed fun. It's a place for all the family.

Encounter close-up meetings with animals from all over the world...

Hand feed wallabies, stroll with Pygmy goats and Cameroon sheep in the African Village (new for 2011). A stroll to the Valley of the Apes to see Steve and Lisa's Baby Bryn is a must.

This conservation-led zoo has one of Europe's largest Lemur Walkthroughs where you will meet five endangered lemur species. And don't forget to take a peek at Meerkat Mountain before relaxing over a glass of wine next to the world's largest bird table.

REAL FUN REAL FOOD REAL EXPERIENCE
Spring, Summer, Autumn, Winter - Manor House offers real food all year round. Some of our Double-Bubblers come just for lunch!

And kids just love the freedom and space - flying the Dragon, bouncing around in the Hay Play Barn, wandering through the Burrow, laughing and learning.

Connect with the wonders of nature... the beautiful parkland, close-up animal experiences, wildlife trails and great food make this the the perfect all-year experience.

ANNA'S WELSH ZOO
Filming continues through 2011 for Anna's Welsh Zoo. the new series will air in the Autumn.

DOUBLE-BUBBLE
The Manor House Season Pass is the hottest ticket in Wales. It's great value - just pay twice the first time you come and the rest of the year is free.

all details can be found on
www.manorhousewildlifepark.co.uk or ring 01646 651201

Lots of laughs and lots to learn - the perfect day out.

'My kids love it, and yours will too!'
Anna x

OAKWOOD THEME PARK

Set in 80 acres of spectacular Pembrokeshire countryside, Oakwood is one of the UK's leading theme parks with more than 30 exhilarating attractions; including four world class rides to enjoy.

Don't miss Megafobia - famed as one of the wildest wooden coasters on the planet, it has been voted the best ride in the UK and the 3rd best ride in the world by coaster enthusiasts from the Roller Coaster Club of Great Britain.

With a top speed in excess of 75 kph and 25 metre drops towards a lake combined with unique crossovers this twister has attained legendary status among coaster fans worldwide.

The park is also home to Drenched the tallest, steepest and wettest ride in Europe, Speed with its awe-inspiring beyond vertical drop and Bounce where riders are shot into the air at up to 70kph in just two seconds!

Plus there's the added thrill of Vertigo* – the skydiver-designed extreme flight experience and the closest thing to flying like an eagle.

The ride provides awesome aerial views of the park and surrounding countryside and can accommodate one, two or three riders simultaneously (*subject to supplementary charge).

Oakwood's unique combination of attractions also includes spectacular family rides, children's themed play areas and so much more.

You can whizz around the watery slides of Snake River Falls, become a pilot on Plane Crazy or take a relaxing paddle on the Boating Lake.

Seek out the spine tingling ghouls on Spooky 3D, plummet down the Waterfall slide, climb aboard the Pirate Ship or take on the hairpins of the Bobsleigh run.

For smaller kids there's KidzWorld with its undercover adventure play world The Lost Kingdom and Wacky Factory.

NEW FOR SUMMER 2011 – WILD WEST HIGH DIVING SHOW!

For the first time ever in Wales come and witness one of the most incredible high diving shows in the world!

Our team of fearless cowboys perform incredible high altitude stunts as part of a Wild West themed outdoor spectacular as they plunge from a 25 metre board into less than three metres of water.

Taking place on selected dates throughout July and August this show is not to be missed!

Oakwood Theme Park, Canaston Bridge, Narberth, Pembrokeshire SA67 8DE. Open from April 2011. For a world class day out call for more information on 01834 891 373 or visit www.oakwoodthemepark.co.uk

OAKWOOD
THEME PARK

BEST FAMILY DAY OUT IN WALES!

RENCHED

NEW WILD WEST DIVE SHOW ★

FAMILY THRILLS!

MEGAFOBIA
THRILLS BEYOND FEAR

★ On selected dates in July and August

www.oakwoodthemepark.co.uk

Canaston Bridge, Narberth, Pembrokeshire, SA67 8DE
Tel: 01834 891373

IF YOU GO DOWN TO THE WOODS TODAY....

you'll encounter over 30 dinosaurs at the Tenby Dinosaur Park.
Complete the free quiz and earn **your** expert sticker when you
finish the mile long walk deep in the woodlands. T-Rex is always
hungry and tiptoe past the spitting Dilosophaur otherwise you
might get wet. Meet the Stegosaurus family and look out for the
hissing Raptors devouring a meal. Take care on the boardwalks
over the swamps, you'll hear all sorts of strange noises and lots
of surprises.

This year we're opening at February half term and looking forward
to seeing old and new friends and you'll only have to pay once as
all the rides are free.

Visit Dino's Den Adventure Indoor Playland with soft play areas
for toddlers and hard play for bigger kids. Computersaurus Alley
offers screens for all ages and skills, with CD Roms and educational games. See live hatchlings in an incubator and examine a
dinosaur egg nest as well as other activities in the Activity
Centre. Dig for your own fossil, identify it, name it and take it
home with you.

Outdoor Play includes the Giant Astra Slide, the Dippy Dinoslide,
Orbiter Car circuit and motorised tractors as well as Disco Boats.
The Jungle Climb and Jurassic challenge will test your skills and
the whole family will enjoy the 18 hole volcanic themed Adventure
Golf and Frisbee Golf. Get your licence on the brilliant 4 x 4 off-
roaders circuit and reach for the sky on the Superjumper trampo-
lines. Little ones will be busy digging in Excavator Alley and
making sandcastles whilst older kids can try their hand with the
grown-up digger. The Family Games Garden is great for all the
family with Dinos & Ladders, Jurassic Jigsaws, Guess Who?,
Roaring Racers and Hoopiasaurus and new for 2011 is the
amazing Bubble Ride.

When you're ready to eat choose from the Rib Cage Restaurant
with toddler sized and family meals or sit on the terrace by the
self-service kiosk - there's something for everyone.

It's great value for a full day out!

BATTLEFIELD LIVE PEMBROKESHIRE

Llanteg
10 mins from Tenby and 15 mins from Carmarthen

Award Winning Activity

Battlefield LIVE is an outdoor combat team game using infra-red (the Royal Marines are currently using these guns for their combat training). Battlefield Live is NOT paintball and NOT tame lasertag. There are no projectiles and therefore no pain or bruising. Our combat games are eye safe and suitable for anyone to play (minimum age is 6), whether you are new to outdoor combat-games or a veteran player. Battlefield LIVE is fun, challenging, and full of adrenaline-pumping action. We specialise in team building and the emphasis is very much on teamwork and strategy. We run Battlefield LIVE in our "jungle" woodland. Players carry out missions that challenge them to assault and hold a base, escort VIP's, retrieve the Flight box, sabotage, sniper, patrol and other military scenarios. Our combat games

SESSION TIMES AND PRICE

MORNING 11am – 1pm
AFTERNOON 2pm – 4pm

In the summertime 5pm - 7pm sessions available in the week.

PRICE IS £20 PER PERSON.

Safety briefing included in each session.

Suitable from age 7.

Deposit is required on booking.

NIGHT OPS

6pm – 7.30pm

£20 PER PERSON
Alternative times on request

Camouflage coveralls designed to blend you in to the surroundings as much as possible.

Camouflage jungle hats or caps onto which two sensors are attached for your opponents to aim at.

Camo face paint.

Footwear is not provided so please ensure you wear suitable boots/shoes for the weather.

All our guns can toggle between semi-auto and full-auto.

run for 2 hours and cost £20 per person. There are no extra charges for ammo. When all your lives are gone your marshall will 'respawn' you straight back into the action.

Everyone is welcome - from single players to large groups. You do not have to be in a big group to book - we join players together.

Battlefield Live is perfect for:-

*A Family Day Out
*Birthday Parties
*Celebrations
*Sports Teams/Clubs
*Corporate Groups

Gamers kit up with weapons and sensors firmly attached to caps/hats and guns. Aiming through red dot or telescopic scopes they shoot a precision infrared beam of light at the opponents' sensors. These flash red to register a hit. When a player runs out of lives the gun deactivates. Sensors shine red continuously so there's no cheating. Action resumes with a rapid respawn from the marshal.

To book please phone
07777 671301
or email:
pembslivegaming@btinternet.com

WE ARE LOCATED JUST OFF THE A477 AT AMROTH ROAD, LLANTEG, SA67 8QJ 10 MINS FROM TENBY AND 15 MINS FROM CARMARTHEN

For more intel check out Facebook page & website:
www.battlefieldlivepembrokeshire.co.uk

65

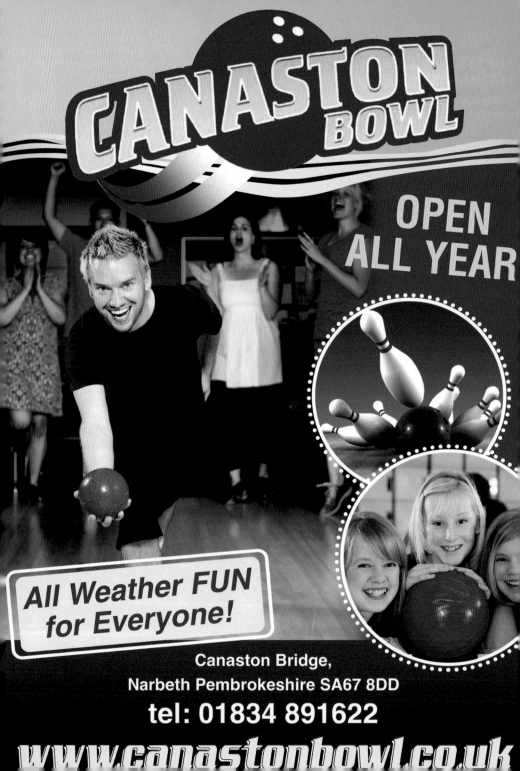

BATTLEFIELD LIVE
Tel: 07777 671301

BLACKPOOL MILL
Tel: 01437 541233

BLUE LAGOON
Tel: 01834 862410

BP KARTING
Tel: 01437 769555

CANASTON BOWL
Tel: 01834 891622

CAREW KARTING
Tel: 01559 384078

CASTELL HENLLYS
Tel: 01239 891319

CWM DERI VINEYARD
Tel: 01834 891274

THE DINOSAUR PARK
Tel: 01834 845272

FOLLY FARM
Tel: 01834 812731

HEATHERTON SPORTS PARK
Tel: 01646 652000

LLYS-Y-FRAN COUNTRY PARK
Tel: 01437 532694

MANOR HOUSE WILD ANIMAL PARK
Tel: 01646 651201

OAKWOOD THEME PARK
Tel: 01834 891373

OCEAN LAB
Tel: 01348 874737

PALACE CINEMA
Tel:01437 767675

RITEC VALLEY QUAD BIKES
Tel: 01834 843390

SCOLTON MANOR
Tel: 01437 731328

TORCH THEATRE
Tel: 01646 695267

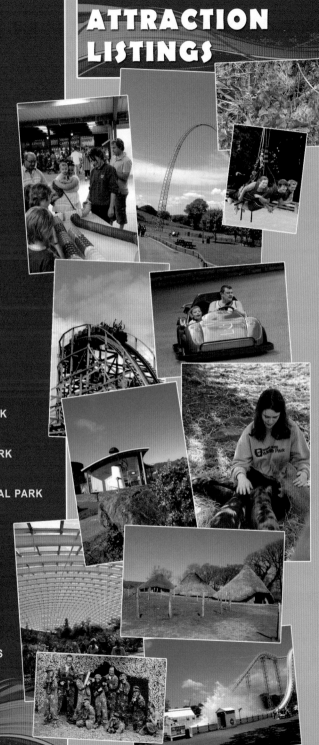

PEMBROKESHIRE & BEYOND
Whatever the weather!

PEMBROKESHIRE & BEYOND
Whatever the weather!

THE WEST COAST

Pembrokeshire's Atlantic West Coast is a wild and dramatic landscape of spectacular cliff scenery, golden beaches and secluded coves. Offshore are the nearby islands of Skomer and Skokholm and much further out to sea, Grassholm, names which are a reminder of the days when ransacking Viking war lords and Norse settlers made their mark in the area. Not surprisingly, Haverfordwest has increasingly become a major holiday base for visitors to the Dale Peninsula, Marloes Peninsula, St. Bride's Bay and even the Preseli Hills. Indeed, it is ideally placed for exploring the whole of Pembrokeshire.

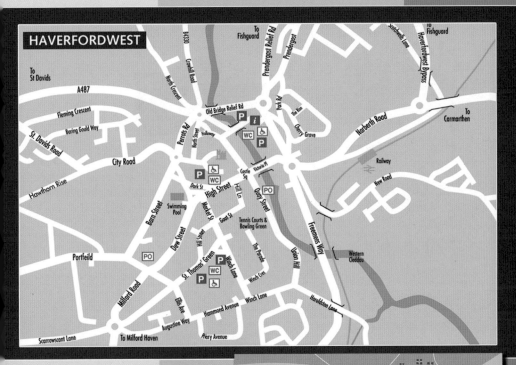

HAVERFORDWEST

Overlooking the town centre are the ruins of the medieval castle. The centre itself has a medieval street plan, but the first appearances suggest that the only buildings older than 18th century are the castle and three Norman churches of St. Mary's, St. Martin's and St. Thomas's. However, behind the new facades of many buildings are much older structures.

PEMBROKESHIRE
County Show

Showtime!

16th, 17th, 18th AUGUST 2011

To be held at:
THE COUNTY SHOWGROUND, WITHYBUSH, HAVERFORDWEST

FURTHER DETAILS:
The General Manager, Show Office, County Showground, Withybush, Haverfordwest, Pembs. SA62 4BW
Tel: 01437 764331 Fax: 01437 767203
email:
info@pembrokeshirecountyshow.co.uk

Riverside Quay, Haverfordwest

The keep and substantial sections of wall are all that remain of the castle today. In the 18th and 19th centuries it was used as a gaol, until the new county gaol was built in 1820. It has also been a police station. St. Mary's Church is one of South Wales' finest. Built in the 13th century but substantially altered in the 15th century, it has many outstanding features, including curved oak roofs, a brass dating back to 1651 and an early English lancet window. St. Martin's with its high steeple, is the town's oldest church and has undergone much restoration. From Tudor times to the early part of this century Haverfordwest was a flourishing port. The decline of the port is a familiar story

in 19th century Wales. In 1853 the arrival of the first train in Haverfordwest was greeted with great celebration. travel had dawned and shipping could not compete. Today, the once hectic quay has become the Riverside Quay Shopping Centre. A modern and attractive development, it includes a large indoor market a reminder that Haverfordwest has for centuries been an important market town. There is a wide range of fresh local produce on sale here, along with locally made crafts and a popular open air Farmer's Market. There is also a large open air market held on Sundays on Withybush airfield.

Haverforwest

HAVERFORWEST TOWN MUSEUM

See Pembrokeshire's Castles and Museums section.

HAVERFORWEST SPORTS CENTRE

tel: 01437 776676

HAVERFORWEST PRIORY

Robert Fitz-Tancred, castellan of Haverforwest, who died in 1213, founded the Augustinian Priory of St. Mary & St. Thomas the Martyr. In 1536, during Henry VIII's Dissolution of the Monasteries, it was stripped of its lead roof and the stonework was plundered. Not surprisingly it became a rich source of building stone, but at various times in later years also fulfilled other roles, such as a boatyard, smithy and stables. The ruins, within easy walking distance of the towns centre are now being excavated by a team of archaeologists working with CADW (Welsh Historic Monuments), and many interesting finds have been made to date.

HAVERFORDWEST TOWN MUSEUM

Haverfordwest is steeped in history. Founded by Flemish migrants circa 1110 the settlement grew into a prosperous medieval borough with strong castle, Augustinian priory, friary and three parish churches. The town was an important port trading with Ireland, Bristol and Continental Europe. During the Middle Ages and well into the seventeenth century Haverfordwest was probably the largest town in Wales. In 1479 a charter was granted by the Prince of Wales (later King Edward V) allowing for the election of a mayor, sheriff and council. The document also conferred county status on the town, the only instance in Welsh history. Being centrally situated in the county of Pembrokeshire, with the river Cleddau flowing through it, the town was well situated to develop into a key market centre, as well as the seat of justice and local administration. Over the centuries the wealth of commerce was expressed in fine buildings and rich endowments to the parish churches. Some of the timber-framed medieval buildings survived into the twentieth century but alas none survive today.

Over the centuries many famous visitors have made their way here. King Henry II was here in 1171, along with other monarchs as King John, Edward I, Richard II, Oliver Cromwell and George IV. During the civil wars (1642-48) the castle changed hands five times although there was only a direct military assault once (1645). Several years later a terrible outbreak of bubonic plague (1652) raged for eight months and killed perhaps 300 townspeople. Georgian Haverfordwest was a place of refinement and elegance boasting cobbled streets, whitewashed cottages and fine townhouses. The place was even dubbed 'Little Bath' on account of its then similarity to that well-known English spa town. Haverfordwest continued to proposer as a shire town even returning its own member of Parliament (1547-1885). In 1853 the arrival of the South Wales Railway signalled a slow decline in the importance of the port. Reflecting nine centuries of history is no easy task. The museum reflects the important themes and people who have written large entries in the pages of history and does so through artefacts, paintings, prints and photographs.

HAVEN COURT

Nestling in a wooded valley, in the picturesque village of Little Haven and just a couple of blocks from the beach, lies Haven Court, in the Pembrokeshire National Park. The apartment complex of Haven Court has been designed to complement the environment. The surrounding coastal area, with its rich historical heritage, offers activities ranging from walking and bird-watching to windsurfing. The village has several cozy Inns.

The apartments are mainly 2 bedroom units sleeping 6 people and a 3 bedroom unit sleeping up to 8. The 2 bedroom apartments have a double bedroom, twin bedroom and sofa bed plus one bathroom with shower over the bath. The 3 bedroom apartments is on two floors with a double bedroom, 2 twin bedrooms and sofa bed, one bathroom and an extra shower room.

All sofa beds are in the living area and convert into a double bed. All apartments are heated and have colour TV and DVD player with freeview channels. They are decorated in a traditional cottage style. The kitchens are fully equipped with a microwave and an electric oven and dishwasher. All the comforts of home while you are on holiday so why not give us a call.

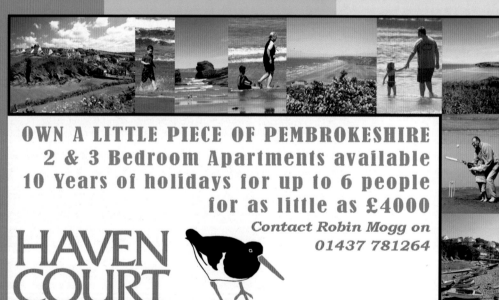

Little Haven

SCOLTON HERITAGE PARK

Within the park's 60 acres of landscaped grounds and woodland stands Scolton House, which dates back to the 1840's and is furnished throughout in the style of the 1920's. New displays in the Victorian stable block illustrate what life was like on a Pembrokeshire country estate, including stabling, cart shed, carpenter's workshop and smithy. Other attractions include an animal enclosure, arboretum, nature trail and a new "green" visitor centre made entirely of local materials.

for more information ring
01437 731328

RHOS

Virtually on the doorstep of this quiet and attractive little village, situated about two miles to the south of the main A40

Haverfordwest to St.Clears road, is the stately Picton Castle. The road through the village also gives you access to the banks of the Eastern Cleddau, an ideal picnic site on a warm Summer's day. Facing you across the water here is the slipway at Landshipping and a few hundred yards to your right is Picton Point, the confluence of the Western and Eastern Cleddau rivers.

LITTLE HAVEN

This is a tiny village resort of great charm and beauty, nestling between high cliffs. The beach, a sandy cove which at low tide connects with neighbouring Broad Haven, is popular with bathers and boaters and visitors to its welcoming pubs and restaurants. It is hard to imagine that coal from local pits was once exported from here.

Little Haven

77

BROAD HAVEN

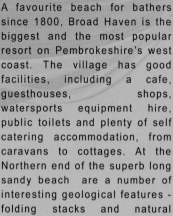

Broad Haven

A favourite beach for bathers since 1800, Broad Haven is the biggest and the most popular resort on Pembrokeshire's west coast. The village has good facilities, including a cafe, guesthouses, shops, watersports equipment hire, public toilets and plenty of self catering accommodation, from caravans to cottages. At the Northern end of the superb long sandy beach are a number of interesting geological features - folding stacks and natural arches.

Broad Haven

WOLF'S CASTLE

Wolf's Castle (also frequently referred to in print as Wolfscastle) is at the northern end of the Treffgarne Gorge, where, in the early part of the century, railwaymen toiled to blast an unlikely route through the very old and very hard rock bed in a bid to fulfil Brunel's dream. A motte and bailey castle stands near the centre of the village, which is popular with holidaymakers by virtue of its inn, hotel and pottery. Archaeological finds nearby include Roman tiles and slates, indicating the site of a fortified Roman-British villa. The village was the birthplace in 1773 of Joseph Harris, who in 1814 published Seren Gomer, the first all Welsh weekly newspaper.

ROCH

Dominating the otherwise flat landscape for miles around, Roch Castle stands on an igneous rock outcrop. The origin of the castle and its large pele tower is unknown, but it is thought that it was built in the 13th century by Adam de Rupe. Legend says that he chose the site because of a prophecy that he would die from an adder's bite. Unluckily for him, an adder was brought into the castle in a bundle of firewood and duly fulfilled the prediction. The small village of Roch has a 19th century church with a circular churchyard.

NEWGALE

A popular surfing resort, newgale is a small village at the north-eastern end of St. Bride's Bay, overlooking the impressive two mile stretch of Newgale Sands. The sands are separated from the road and village by a high ridge of pebbles. At exceptionally low tides the stumps of a drowned prehistoric forest are sometimes exposed.

TREFFGARNE

Treffgarne was the birthplace of the rebellious Welsh hero Owain Glyndwr. The village stands close to the wooded rocky gorge, through which runs the Western Cleddau river, railway line and main A40 trunk road. The Treffgarne Gorge was cut by meltwater rushing south towards Milford Haven during the retreat of the last Ice Age. The areas around the gorge are dotted with sites of early settlements and fortifications, and on the western side rises the igneous outcrop of Great Treffgarne Mountain and other striking rock formations.

NANT-Y-COY MILL

Restored Nant y Coy Mill dates back to 1332 and possibly even earlier. The last corn was ground here in the 1950's, but the mill wheel is still turning 150

years after it was built. With a nature trail leading up to the Great Treffgarne Rocks, from where the views of the gorge are spectacular. You can also take a detour to Lion Rock and Bear Rock, two of the most distinctive features of the Pembrokeshire landscape.

NOLTON HAVEN

This compact coastal village, with its attractive cove, is virtually midway between little Haven and Newgale. In the 18th century, coal was exported from here, and the the line of the tramway which brought the anthracite and coal from the mines to the coast can still be seen. Alongside the old track bed is the Counting House, which recorded how many wag-onloads of coal were transported to the quay. The quay itself, built in 1769, no longer exists. Half a mile north of Nolton Haven was Trefran Cliff Colliery, which worked coal seams beneath St. Bride's Bay between 1850 and 1905. Part of an old chimney and other ruins are now the only evidence of this once thriving industry.

Nolton Haven

Newgale

79

RUDBAXTON

Rudbaxton is about 2 miles north of Haverfordwest and is the site of one of the region's most impressive earthworks, a motte and bailey fortress established in the 11th century. In a valley below the mound is the parish church of St. Michael. This dates from the 12th century and was restored in the 1870's.

MILFORD HAVEN

DISTANCES: Fishguard 24m, Haverfordwest 7m, Narberth 15m, Pembroke 7m, St. Davids 21m, Tenby 17m, Carmarthen 37m and London 253m

Since its development as a new town and whaling port in the late 18th century, Milford Haven has seen its economic fortunes seesaw. Sir William Hamilton, husband of Nelson's Emma, was granted an Act of Parliament to proceed with the development of the town and port, and from the beginning it was envisaged that new Milford would secure its share of the transatlantic shipping trade. Assisted by

Milford Haven

settlers from overseas, progress was rapid, with the early establishment of a quay, custom house, inn and naval dockyard. When Nelson visited in 1802 he was suitably impressed with the development and the Haven waterway, which he described as "one of the worlds finest natural harbours".During the mid 1800's, a renewed effort was made to re-establish Milford Haven as a transatlantic staging post, and ambitious plans were drawn up for the building of docks to rival those at Liverpool and Southampton. Although these never materialised, the far more modest Milford Haven docks opened in 1888. New life was breathed into the new docks, when the first vessel to enter was the steam trawler Sybil on the 27th September 1888. Her arrival marked the beginning of a prosperous new era for Milford Haven as the port turned its attention to deep-sea fishing.

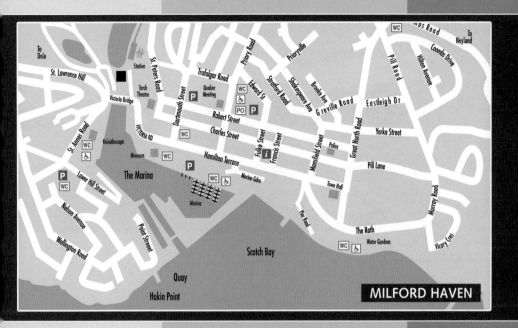

Map labels: To Dale · St. Lawrence Hill · Station · St Peters Road · Torch Theatre · Victoria Bridge · VICTORIA RD · Dartmouth Street · Quaker Meeting · Trafalgar Road · Priory Road · Prioryville · Prioryville · Shakespeare Ave · Stratford Road · Edward St · Brooke Ave · Greville Road · Eastleigh Dr · Pill Road · Hilton Avenue · Coombs Drive · To Ney'land · Kaleidoscope · St. Annes Road · Museum · Charles Street · Robert Street · Fulke Street · Francis Street · Mansfield Street · Great North Road · Yorke Street · Police · Pill Lane · Hamilton Terrace · The Marina · Lower Hill Street · Nelson Avenue · Point Street · Wellington Road · Marina · Marine Gdns · Town Hall · The Rath · Murray Road · Vicary Cres · Water Gardens · Scotch Bay · Quay · Hakin Point · PO · WC

MILFORD HAVEN

The combination of new docks, excellent fishing grounds and good rail links saw the enterprise reap rich rewards. In its heyday in the 1920's, the port was home to 130 deep sea trawlers which offered employment to around 4,000 men either afloat or ashore. By the 1950's the seesaw had tipped the other way again as the fishing industry slipped into an irretrievable decline. This time however, the promise of yet another new beginning for Milford Haven was already in the pipeline, the coming of the oil industry. In recent years this industry too has had its ups and downs. Despite the industry's problems the wealth generated by oil has helped fund Milford Haven's massive new investment in tourism. This has seen the complete refurbishment of the old docks and the creation of the superb 150 berth marina. Many of the old buildings have been demolished, while others of historic significance have been renovated and now house such attractions as the museum. A thriving retail and business park has been developed which has attracted many new business to the docks area.

Milford Haven

81

Milford Marina

"Spirit of Adventure"

"Amadea" courtesy of David Barrett

Milford Haven Port Authority has become an important name in the development of cruise opportunities for Pembrokeshire and Wales. Working with Welsh and Irish partners, the Authority is playing an important role in marketing the Celtic sea and its family of ports as some of Europe's best cruising destinations

Milford Haven has become a popular port of call for many cruise lines, with the number of boutique passenger vessels increasing each year. European, American and British passengers step ashore at Milford, keen to explore the history and culture of Pembrokeshire. From St Davids Cathedral and the Castles of Pembroke and Carew to the tranquil shopping at Narberth, Pembroke and Milford, a diversity of excursion opportunities are showcasing the best that our county has to offer.

"Black Watch" courtesy of Pembrokeshire Photography

Our cruise calls are increasing year by year and for 2011 we will have 9 calls, with bookings already coming in for 2012.

For more information contact:
Sue Blanchard-Williams
Cruise and Event Coordinator
sue.blanchard@mhpa.co.uk
www.mhpa.co.uk
Tel: 01646 696100

Milford Haven Port Authority

TORCH THEATRE
MILFORD HAVEN

Milford Haven's Torch Theatre celebrated its 30th anniversary in 2007 with an ambitious refurbishment project which transformed it into one of the most comfortable venues in the British Isles.

The striking new theatre was re-launched in the spring of 2008 with a sell-out production of the award-winning musical *The Hired Man*. The Torch has its own celebrated professional producing theatre company and boasts an impressive repertoire of over 160 productions, including *One Flew Over The Cuckoo's Nest, Neville's Island, Abigail's Party, The Little Shop of Horrors, Of Mice and Men, Educating Rita, The Norman Conquests*, a highly acclaimed co-production of *She Stoops to Conquer* which also toured the UK and, most recently, *Intimate Exchanges* and *An Inspector Calls*. Their Christmas show is always a firm family favourite and you can also catch first rate touring shows ranging from musical theatre, plays and comedy to dance, opera, lectures and the best in live music.

Every day there is a busy programme of films, including the latest movie blockbusters, family movies, children's matinees, the classics and off-beat films - so there is always an option for those days when the sun forgets to put his hat on...

Café Torch is a welcoming place for friends and family to enjoy good, home-made food in a relaxed and friendly setting. Opening onto a cliff top terrace, the Café has panoramic views over Milford's marina and docks and also has free WiFi access. The Torch has entertained thousands of children over the years, so it makes sense that they are family friendly at Cafe Torch as well. Childs portions are available and they also have highchairs and baby changing facilities There is also a lovely Bar upstairs, with its own terrace to relax on.

Sitting conveniently alongside Café Torch is the vibrant *Joanna Field Gallery* exhibiting the best of Pembrokeshire's buoyant art scene, including painting, photography, crafts, ceramics, multimedia, installations and sculpture. Entry is free.

An Inspector Calls

Cinderella

To find out what's on, call the Box Office on 01646 695267 or visit their website www.torchtheatre.co.uk where you can also purchase tickets.

MILFORD HAVEN HERITAGE & MARITIME MUSEUM

OPENING TIMES:
LATE MARCH - MID OCTOBER
MON - SAT: 11.00 - 16.00

SPECIAL ARRANGEMENTS
CAN BE MADE FOR PARTIES
AND GROUPS

ADMISSION FEES:
ADULTS £1.50
CONCESSIONARY RATE: £1.00

Milford Haven is an unusual town, developed by Quaker Whalers from New England. In the late 19th Century, a dock system was built in the hope of breaking into the Transatlantic Liner Trade. The home of a major fishing industry. As the fishing industry declined in the 1950's, its place was taken by the oil industry. The museum tells this historical story with models, artifacts, sound and pictures.

**THE OLD
CUSTOM HOUSE,
SYBIL WAY, MILFORD
MARINA, MILFORD
HAVEN, SA73 3AF
TEL: 01646 694496**

NEYLAND

Neyland

Like Milford Haven, Neyland has been revitalised by the building of an impressive new marina and waterfront development, Brunel Quay. Its name could only be a reference to the great railway engineer, whose aim was to establish Neyland as a prosperous transatlantic port by choosing it as the terminus of the South Wales Railway. An impressive statue of Brunel now stands at the entrance to Brunel Quay in recognition of his achievements. At one time or another during the 18th and 19th centuries, virtually every port and resort on the entire Welsh coast had designs on winning the battle for the highly lucrative transatlantic trade. In that year the service was transferred to Fishguard in the north of the county. The railway remained operational until 1964 when the town's depot was closed.The route of the old railway line now provides an enjoyable country walk between the marina and the village of Rosemarket. Mountain bikers can also tackle the 14m circular Brunel Cycle Route.

HERBRANDSTON

Located approximately 3 miles north west of Milford Haven and just off the main road to Dale/Marloes, Herbrandston is a pretty village with post office/store, village pub and church. The vilage derives its name from one of the Norman or Flemish settlers in Pembrokeshire named Herbrand who, soon after the Conquest, made his home here.

ST. ISHMAELS

Located between Milford Haven and Dale, the village of St. Ishmaels lies in a deep sheltered valley. Nearby are important historical sites, a Norman motte and bailey to the north and the Iron Age forts of Great and Little Castle Heads to the east. The 12th century church stands away from the village, on the site where St. Ishmael is believed to have founded his principle church in the 6th century. A stream divides the churchyard.

DALE

This one time shipbuilding and trading port is now one of the most popular sailing centres in Pembrokeshire and has good facilities for visitors. Races are held on most days during the summer and in August there is a regatta. Close to the village is Dale Fort, one of the Victorian defences built to protect the waterway and is now used as a geographical field study centre. At the western end of the village, the road leads to the magnificent St Ann's Head, with its lighthouse and coastguard station from where there are stunning views of the Haven waterway and its busy shipping lanes.

Marloes

MARLOES

This pretty little village with its attractive cottages and church lies en-route to Marloes Sands, off the B4327. Marloes Sands can be reached from the village or from Dale. The panoramic views above the beach take in the islands of Skomer, Skokholm and the much smaller Grassholm, which at low tide can be reached from the northern end of the beach. The road through Marloes village also gives you access to the peaceful cove of Martin's Haven, the departure point for Skomer Island and other island boat trips.

Marloes

Dale

SPORT & LEISURE ACTIVITIES

Health and fitness are increasingly important facets of modern lifestyles, and this is reflected in the growing number of visitors who come in great numbers to Pembrokeshire in search of sporting and activity holidays. Certainly there is no better place to choose, with the only coastline in Britain designated a National Park, Pembrokeshire combines the best of the great outdoors with the very best in indoor leisure facilities.

Activity Centres

Heddfan,
Blockett Lane
Little Haven
SA62 3UH

BASE CAMP OUTDOOR CENTRE

Llawhaden, Narberth
Offers canoeing and kayaking, climbing
and abseiling, walking and hillwalking.

PEMBROKESHIRE WATER SPORTS

Ahoy Pembrokeshire,
15 Church Road,
Hazelbeach,
Milford Haven
SA73 1EB

CELTIC DIVING

The Parrog, Goodwick
Offers diving, snorkelling courses,
refresher dives and boat trips.

DIVE PEMBROKESHIRE

Gelli Cottage
Ludchurch
Narberth
SA67 8LE

THE PRINCES TRUST

Pembrokeshire Adventure Centre
Cleddau Reach
Pembroke Dock
SA72 6UJ

FFOREST OUTDOOR

Bridge Warehouse, Teifi Wharf,
Cardigan, SA43 3AA
Clothing and accessories for a range of
outdoor sports
including climbing, walking, kayaking
and canoeing

WEST WALES WIND, SURF
AND SAILING

Dale
Canoeing, kayaking, surfing, sailing,
windsurfing and
powerboats. Caters for
wheelchair users

Skomer Island

BIRDWATCHING

Puffins

Ardent twitchers or those who just enjoy watching birds can have the time of their lives whatever the season. In winter the rivers Teifi, Cleddau and Nevern are home to Little Egrets, Slovonian Grebes and Great Northern Divers, together with Wildfowl Waders. Spring sees the arrival of swallows, warblers and many varieties of seabirds, while inland Peregrine falcons, Merlins, together with Lapwings, Golden Plovers and Buzzards take to the sky. The islands of Ramsey, Skomer and Grassholm offer the widest selection of birds including Fulmars, Kittiwakes, Guillemots, Razorbills and Puffins to name but a few. Skomer has the distinction of being home to the largest colony of Manx Shearwaters in the world, while Grassholm has the second largest colony of Gannets in the North Atlantic. Elegug Stacks near Castlemartin also has large colonies of Guillemots, Razorbills and Kittiwakes, while the Welsh Wildlife Centre at Cilgerran near Cardigan is home to countless varieties of birds and wildfowl. Both Skomer and Ramsey can be visited by boat. Skomer boats run daily (except Mondays, excluding Bank Holidays) from Martins Haven between April 1st or Easter, which ever is sooner, until October 31st.

Contact Dale Sailing Company tel: 01646 603123/603110 There are a number of boat operators who visit Ramsey, contact Voyages of Discovery on 0800 854367 and 01437 721911 or Thousand Islands on 01437 721721, or pick up leaflets locally.

A number of the boat operators also visit Grassholm, where you can't go ashore. Vantage points for bird watching include Amroth, Strumble Head, Nevern Estuary, Cleddau Estuary, Carew Mill Pond, Fishguard Harbour, Westfield Pill at Neyland and Bosherston Lily Ponds near Pembroke.

CANOEING AND KAYAKING

North Pembrokeshire's dramatic coastline offers just the sort of conditions ideal for canoeing and kayaking. For beginners there are quiet sheltered bays where even the complete novice soon feels at home, while the more expert can take up the challenge of tide races and overfalls. Beginners are often surprised to discover that even on their first trip, under the guidance of an experienced and qualified instructor, they begin to master the basic skills and are able to enjoy the thrills of exploring cliffs and sea caves and negotiating rocks and waves.

TYF ADVENTURE
1, High Street, St. Davids.
tel: 01437 721611
Freshwater East.
tel:01646 672764
freephone 0800 132588

PEMBROKESHIRE WATERSPORTS
The Cleddau River Centre,
Pembroke Dock.
tel: 01646 622013
The Parrog, Fishguard.
tel: 01348 874803

FFOREST OUTDOOR
Bridge Warehouse, Teifi
Wharf, Cardigan,
SA43 3AA
tel: 01239 62 36 33
www.fforestoutdoor.co.uk

CLIMBING

Pembrokeshire offers climbers of all abilities the opportunity to experience some of the finest sea cliff climbing in the British Isles. The county's geographical location and mild winters mean all year round climbing on dry, warm rock, a treat rarely available in mountainous areas. So the area is very popular, especially during early bank holidays, and there may well be queues for some of the plum 3 star routes. The sea cliffs are the home of many nesting birds, some of them rare and because of this very necessary restrictions have been imposed in certain areas from early February until mid August. So climbers are advised to choose their routes carefully as it cannot be stressed too strongly that if climbers and wildlife are to co-exist successfully in this environmentally sensitive corner of Britain, the restrictions imposed must be adhered to. Further details of these restrictions are available from all National Park Information Centres and in the Climbers Guide to Pembrokeshire.

DAILY SURF REPORTS
WHITESANDS
www.masimes.co.uk

NEWGALE
www.newsurf.co.uk

WILD WEST WALES
www.aswildasyouwantit.com

PEMBROKESHIRE
www.surfwithus.co.uk
www.pembrokeshireactive.co.uk

BROAD HAVEN
www.outerreefsurfschool.com
www.havensports.co.uk

PEMBROKESHIRE
WATER ACTIVITIES
www.princes-trust.org.uk
www.touristnetuk.com
www.pembrokeshire-wales.info
www.pembrokeshirewatersports.co.uk
www.pembrokeshire-sports.co.uk
www.dive-pembrokeshire.com
www.activitywales.com

EQUIPMENT HIRE
www.pembrokeshireboatcharters.com
www.havensports.co.uk
www.tenbymarine.co.uk
www.surfdale.co.uk
www.masimes.co.uk

COURSES
www.outerreefsurfschool.com
www.whitesandssurfschool.co.uk
www.tyf.com
www.celticdiving.co.uk

FFOREST OUTDOOR

Bridge Warehouse, Teifi Wharf,
Cardigan, SA43 3AA
tel: 01239 62 36 33
www.fforestoutdoor.co.uk

Fforest Outdoor has West Wales' largest selection of equipment, clothing and accessories for a range of outdoor sports including climbing, walking, kayaking and canoeing, with over 35 boats of all shapes and sizes in stock. From our waterside location you can try before you buy on our entire range, book on a variety of activities, hire a mountain bike or just take a quiet coffee and cake in our dedicated adventure café! Find us by the old bridge in the centre of Cardigan.

CYCLING AND MOUNTAIN BIKING

There is no better way to enjoy the magnificence of the Pembrokeshire coastline and the beauty and tranquillity of the countryside than on a bike, especially as the whole of the National Park is crisscrossed with a network of hidden tracks, bridle ways and sunken lanes. When cycling in Pembrokeshire it is very important to remember that the coast path is for walkers only, a law strictly enforced by the National Park Authority, who are responsible for maintaining this long distance footpath. Furthermore, off road cyclists should give way at all times to walkers and horse riders, and be courteous and considerate to the farmers and landowners whose land they are crossing. For cyclists who prefer to be on the road than off it Pembrokeshire has more quiet lanes than most people could cycle round in a lifetime. Touring in the county could hardly be easier, with bed and breakfast available round every corner and plenty of youth hostels within easy reach.

COASTEERING

Another growing sport is Coasteering, which is definitely an activity for the more daring. It involves a combination of climbing and scrambling along the rocky coastline, swimming and cliff jumping into the sea.

91

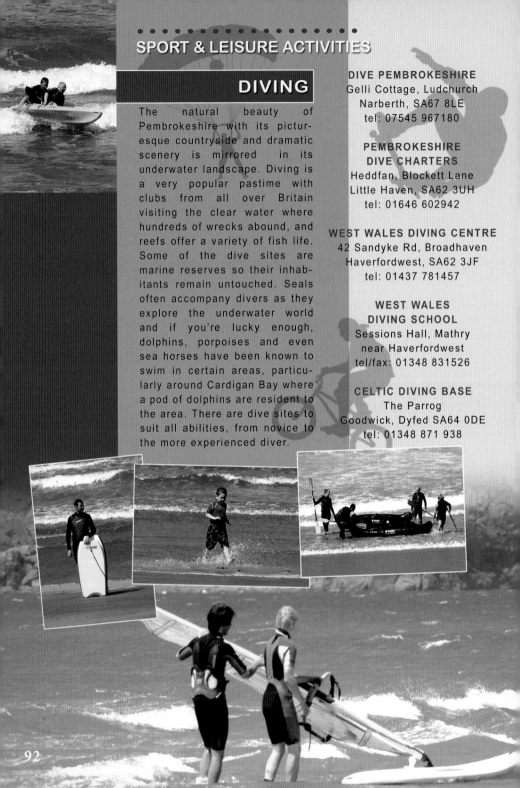

DIVING

The natural beauty of Pembrokeshire with its picturesque countryside and dramatic scenery is mirrored in its underwater landscape. Diving is a very popular pastime with clubs from all over Britain visiting the clear water where hundreds of wrecks abound, and reefs offer a variety of fish life. Some of the dive sites are marine reserves so their inhabitants remain untouched. Seals often accompany divers as they explore the underwater world and if you're lucky enough, dolphins, porpoises and even sea horses have been known to swim in certain areas, particularly around Cardigan Bay where a pod of dolphins are resident to the area. There are dive sites to suit all abilities, from novice to the more experienced diver.

DIVE PEMBROKESHIRE
Gelli Cottage, Ludchurch
Narberth, SA67 8LE
tel: 07545 967180

**PEMBROKESHIRE
DIVE CHARTERS**
Heddfan, Blockett Lane
Little Haven, SA62 3UH
tel: 01646 602942

WEST WALES DIVING CENTRE
42 Sandyke Rd, Broadhaven
Haverfordwest, SA62 3JF
tel: 01437 781457

**WEST WALES
DIVING SCHOOL**
Sessions Hall, Mathry
near Haverfordwest
tel/fax: 01348 831526

CELTIC DIVING BASE
The Parrog
Goodwick, Dyfed SA64 0DE
tel: 01348 871 938

FISHING

Whether you are looking for an out and out fishing holiday or you simply want to enjoy a bit of fishing while you're here, Pembrokeshire and West Wales provide wonderful opportunities for sea, game and coarse fishing. The coastlines of Pembrokeshire, Cardigan Bay and Carmarthen Bay are excellent venues for summer sea angling, either from the beach or from established rock marks. Bass, pollack, garfish, mackerel, conger eel and even tope are all here for the taking, while if you want to fish offshore, there is no shortage of charter boats offering fishing trips from local harbours. West Wales has long been renowned for the quality of its game fishing, with most of the area's rivers and their tributaries experiencing good runs of salmon and sea trout during the summer months. Indeed, the region boasts three of Britain's premier salmon rivers, the Towy, Teifi and Taf, and many others provide terrific sport when conditions are favourable. These include the Nevern, Aeron, Eastern Cleddau, Western Cleddau, Rheidol and Ystwyth. Wales also has an abundance of lakes and reservoirs that are well stocked with brown and rainbow trout. Venues popular with visitors are the reservoirs at Llys-y-fran Country Park and Rosebush, both close to the B4329 about six miles from Haverfordwest, White House Mill and Latch y Goroff, (near Whitland) and the fisheries of Llwyndrissi, Llanllawddog and Garnffrwd, (near Carmarthen). For coarse anglers there are exciting prospects at a variety of locations. Bosherston Lakes offer excellent pike fishing and Llyn Carfan Lake at Tavernspite boasts top class carp fishing and a good head of tench and roach. Glas Llyn fishery near Blaenwaen is also stoked with carp and tench. But remember, anyone over 12 years old who fishes for salmon, trout, freshwater fish or eels in England and Wales must have an Environmental Agency rod fishing licence, available from the Post Office or Environment Agency offices. In addition, you must have permission from the fishery owner before you may fish on waters under their control, and remember to take your litter home, as discarded tackle can injure wildlife.

PENRALLT NURSERY
MOYLEGROVE
tel: 01239 881295

LLYS-Y-FRAN RESERVOIR &
COUNTRY PARK
tel: 01427 532273/532694
see advert page 149

Pembrokeshire Coast
NATIONAL PARK

The Pembrokeshire Coast National Park, one of Britain's breathing spaces, takes in about a third of the county including the entire coastal strip, the upper reaches of the Daugleddau (two swords) and the Preselis. It's the only National Park that is almost all coastal. The National Park run an extensive programme of activities and events for both adults and children: rockpool safaris, crab catching, bat walks and even time travel.

Britain's Only Coastal National Park.

It covers a third of Pembrokeshire including thePreseli Mountains and the upper reaches of the Daugleddau Estuary.

Tenby, St Davids, Saundersfoot, Newport and Manorbier are all in the National Park.

So are Skomer, Skokholm, Caldey and Ramsey Islands. Two inland areas are also in the National Park, The Preseli Mountains and the upper reaches of the Daugleddau Estuary.

The Preseli Mountains are where the Stonehenge bluestones are supposed to have come from.

The Daugleddau Estuary is known, locally, as the secret waterway.

WALKING ROUTES

The best known footpath is the Pembrokeshire Coast Path, which winds its way around the magnificent bays and spectacular headlands. The 186 mile, 299km trek is a strenuous undertaking if you want to complete the route from start to finish.

DINAS ISLAND is a rocky headland near Fishguard. Start at either Cwm yr Eglwys or Pwllgwaelod and take the coast path around the island, returning to your start point via the low lying valley that connects it to the mainland. Total distance covered is about 3 miles or 5km. Catch the Poppit Rocket the walker's bus.

CARREGWASTAD POINT Start in the pretty village of Llanwnda, near Fishguard and backtrack along the road for 1/4 mile before cutting across country towards the ferry terminal at Goodwick. Pick up the coast path and follow it round to Carregwastad Point. If you want to turn back here the distance is about 5 miles or 9km. To carry on to Strumble Head will double the distance. Catch the Strumble Shuttle the walker's bus.

CEMAES HEAD is a rugged and wild section of intensely folded high cliffs. Start at the car park at Poppit near St. Dogmael's and walk up the road past the youth hostel. Follow the coast path to Ceibwr Bay, a distance of 5.5m/7km. By the time you've returned, across country, you'll have covered 9 miles or 16km. Catch the Poppit Rocket the walker's bus.

From the National Park car park at MANORBIER BEACH, below the castle, two walks are available, one going west to the secluded Swanlake Bay a distance of 3miles/5km. The path to the east provides a short circular walk returning through the village. Local Bus Service 349/359

95

STRUMBLE HEAD is a wild and unpopulated stretch of the path with some spectacular cliffs. Start at the car park at Garn Fawr, 2 miles south of Strumble Head and follow winding country lanes all the way to Strumble lighthouse. Continue along the coast path to the Youth Hostel at Pwll Deri and return to the car park via the hilltop where you get magnificent views of the Pen Caer peninsula you've just walked around. Total distance 5 miles, 9km. Catch the Strumble Shuttle the walker's bus.

Either start at ABEREIDDY or at PORTHGAIN, a safe—haven harbour with a good pub and restaurant. There's plenty of interest on the way includ—ing old stone quarries, the Blue Lagoon — a flooded slate quarry and the secret beach of Traeth Llyfn. Returning to your starting point via Barry Island Farm and Felindre House. Total distance is 4 miles/6km. Catch the Strumble Shuttle the walkers bus.

ST. DAVIDS PENINSULA Start behind the Cathedral and follow the lanes north along the valley. When you reach Treleddyd Fawr continue across country until you reach the coast path which you can then follow all the way round the peninsular to Caerfai before returning to St. Davids. This route cover 15miles, 23km or it can be tackled in smaller sections: Whitesands to St. Davids Head and back via Carn Llidi 4 miles/6km Porthstinian to Porthclais and return on the country roads 6miles/10km St. Davids to Porthclais and return via Caerfai 2miles/3km. Catch the Celtic Coaster the walker's bus (summertime only)

Thanks to the introduction of the PUFFIN SHUTTLE between St. Davids and Milford Haven, some excellent stretches of the coast path can now be tackled without the need to do a circular route. Use the shuttle to travel to the far end of your day's walk and walk back to where you started. Good sections to tackle in this fashion include: Solva to St Davids•Newgale to Solva•Little Haven to Nolton Haven•St Brides Haven to Little Haven •Dale to Martins Haven

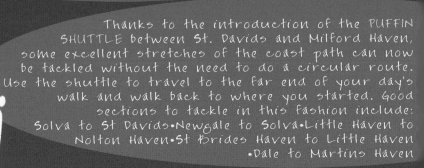

Take a circular route around the MARLOES PENINSULA, starting at either Marloes beacon or the National Trust car park for Marloes beach. It covers a distance of 6.5miles/11km

Another good circular route is around the DALE PENINSULA, starting from the car park near St. Ann's head. The path follows some dramatic cliff tops, dropping down to several lovely sandy coves on the way. Total distance is about 6miles/10km.

SOUTH OF MILFORD HAVEN, another circular route is possible around the Angle Peninsula, starting from either Freshwater West or from West Angle Bay. Travelling in a clockwise direction, you are treated to one of the most dramatic views in Britain as you come over the ridge and see the magnificent beach at Freshwater West stretching away into the distance. Total distance is around 9miles/15km.

The coast path between STACK ROCKS and BROAD HAVEN SOUTH is only acces- sible when the army ranges are open. It's a fascinating stretch of coast but can't be easily incorporated into a circular route because the ranges get in the way. Some unusual rock features, arches, stacks, caves and hidden beaches as well as a visit to St. Govan's Chapel make the walk interesting. Distance one way is 4 miles/7 km. Catch the Coastal Cruiser bus

STACKPOLE QUAY is the start point for a good walk that takes in dramatic cliffs, the lily ponds at Bosherston and one of the most remarkably unspoilt beaches in Britain, Barafundle. As with the previous walk, there isn't a circular option, merely retrace your steps. With teashops at both ends, Stackpole Quay and Bosherston Village, dehydration shouldn't be a problem. Total distance 4 miles/7km. Catch the Coastal Cruiser bus

The coast path from TENBY to SAUNDERSFOOT passes some of the best beaches you're likely to find in Britain including Glen beach, Monkstone and Waterwynch. There's a regular bus service between the towns, the best way to organise a circular route. To walk the route from one direction from harbour to harbour is around 4 miles/6km.
Local bus Service 350/351

LLYS—Y—FRAN COUNTRY PARK. Approximately 7.5 miles, 11km around the reservoir, focal point of the Country Park which has car parks on each side of the lake. Picnic sites, visitor centre, licensed restaurant, toilets, exhibitions area and shops available. Special events and guided walks are also arranged. These include a tour of the reservoir, woodland bird spotting, the chance to try fly fishing and children activities days (including a boat trip). Tel: 01437 532273/532694 for details.

From SAUNDERSFOOT to AMROTH the coast path follows an old tramway, which takes in a series of tunnels for the first mile. The route there and back is approx 5 miles/8km. Local bus service 350/351

Walkers Coastal Bus Services
www.pembrokeshire.gov.uk/coastbus

Walking ideas
www.visitpembrokeshire.com/walking

Pembrokeshire Coast Path National Trail
www.visitpembrokeshire.com/coastpath

Pembrokeshire Coast National Park
www.pembrokeshirecoast.org.uk/walking

The Preseli Circle & Greenways
walking holidays
www.greenwaysholidays.com

Beach wheelchair hire
www.pembrokeshire-access.org.uk

Catering for all the family

Pembrokeshire is a perfect holiday destination for you and your furry friend. With over 50 beaches and 186 miles of the Pembrokeshire Coastal path, there is always somewhere interesting for walkies!

Beaches with dog restrictions between 1st May & 30th September

Lydstep Haven – the western end of the beach
Newgale – between the two main car parks
Saundersfoot – between the harbour and The Strand
Tenby North Beach and The Harbour – all of it
Tenby Castle and South Beaches – from Castle Hill as far as South Beach car park
Amroth – all but the eastern end of the beach
Whitesands – the whole beach
Poppit – from the entrance to the car park directly north over the dunes and beach
Dale – from the car park to the rocks away from the village
Broad Haven (St Brides Bay)-The northern half of the beach

Golf Courses

DERLLYS COURT GOLF CLUB

A delightful 18 hole treelined course of parkland nature, set in beautiful Carmarthenshire countryside with easy access off the bypass between Carmarthen and St. Clears.

for more information
tel: 01267 211575

TENBY GOLF CLUB

Tenby hosts the oldest golf club in Wales where the Burrows offers a superb 18 hole links course. Overlooking Caldey Island, the clubhouse has a restaurant together with bar, lounge and snooker room.

tel: 01834 842978

TREFLOYNE GOLF COURSE

Trefloyne is a family owned golf course, located in the small village of Penally just outside Tenby. Trefloyne offers guests an 18 hole challenging parkland course set in mixed woodlands.

visit us at www.trefloyne.com

ST. DAVIDS CITY GOLF CLUB

Established in 1902, this is one of the oldest golf clubs in Wales, and certainly the most westerly. The all weather links course is playable all year round.

for more information ring the clubhouse
tel: 01437 721751

SOUTH PEMBROKESHIRE GOLF CLUB

This 18 hole hillside course is located at Pembroke Dock, on an elevated site overlooking the River Cleddau and the beautiful Haven Waterway.

for more information
call tel: 01646 621453

MILFORD HAVEN GOLF CLUB

A superb 18 hole par 71 meadowland course, with panoramic views of the Haven Waterway.
tel: 01646 697762

PRISKILLY FOREST GOLF CLUB

Priskilly Forest near Letterston is a nine hole course set in mature parkland and only a ten minute drive from the Stena Ferry terminal at Fishguard.
tel: 01348 840276

ROSEMARKET GOLF COURSE

Rosemarket offers a challenging and very long nine hole parkland course cursed with numerous sand and water hazards to test players.

HEATHERTON & HERONS BROOK GOLF COURSES

Other golf courses include one at St. Florence, an 18 hole pitch and putt course situated at the Heatherton Sports Park, tel: 01646 651025, and the 18 and 9 hole courses at the Heron's Brook Golf and Fishing Retreat in Narberth
tel: 01834 869209

NEWPORT GOLF CLUB

Newport Golf Club & Dormy House Holiday Flats: here you have a golf course which overlooks the magnificent coastline of Newport Bay. The clubhouse offers full catering facilities, and accommodation.
tel: 01239 820244
or visit
www.newportlinks.co.uk

SPORT & LEISURE ACTIVITIES

SYCAMORES RANCH
WESTERN
RIDING CENTRE
Near Llawhaden, Narberth

Have you ever dreamed of riding a western horse on the American plains but thought it was either too expensive or too far to travel?. Well Sycamores Ranch in Llawhaden near Narberth can offer you this experience here in beautiful Wales. The comfortable saddles, well behaved horses, idyllic scenery all add up to an opportunity not to be missed. The Ranch caters for people from the average to the more experienced rider and offer from one hour to whole day trails with barbecue. The trails include riding along quiet offroad bridle paths to crossing rivers, streams and fords. Passing through the delightful Pembrokeshire countryside you will also come across many historical monuments, ranging from ancient castles to traditional Welsh farmhouses and picturesque churches. They also arrange night rides in the summer months. These consist of leaving the Ranch early evening and riding out to a stop off point where a meal is provided, and then riding back to the Ranch in time to put the horses to bed. As well as the trail side they also teach people western riding for those who want to take it a bit more seriously and they also take in horses for backing and schooling in western. The Ranch also has its beautiful American Quarter Horse stallion standing at stud and a Western Tack Shop, which has possibly the largest selection of Western Tack from saddles to Stetsons in Wales.

for more information
visit
www.sycamoresranch.com

KARTING

BP KARTING
County Showground,
Withybush,
Haverfordwest
tel: 01437 769555
see advert page 74

CAREW KARTING
Carew Airfield,
Sageston, Nr Tenby
tel: 07974 540689
01559 384078
see advert page 103

QUAD BIKING

RITEC VALLEY
BUGGIES
Penally, Nr Tenby
tel: 01834 843390
see advert on page 25

102

CAREW Karting

OPEN ALL YEAR

Arrive & Drive

57

58

Grand Prix Events
Children's karts available

500m outdoor tarmac track

Thunder KARTS

THE FASTEST in the business!

Find us **AT CAREW AIRFIELD SA70 8SX**
Tel: **07974 540689**   www.carewkarting.co.uk

LARGEST AND MOST EXCITING KART TRACK IN PEMBROKESHIRE

At Carew karting, we have everything for a great family day out!

We have a 500m outdoor tarmac circuit, top of the range junior karts for children (aged 8 upwards and over 1.35m) and a fleet of brand new Thunder karts for our adult sessions.

We accept individuals and groups

We have a computerized timing system that the whole family can experience the exciting world of racing---- feel the adrenalin buzz

We provide the use of free protective clothing; include a full safety briefing for all competitors and a printout of lap times are given to each driver at the end of their session.. Sensible footwear must be worn (no sandals etc)

We cater for Arrive and drive sessions for adults and children, Corporate and Group Bookings for adults. We have a variety of events from F1 races to Super Grand Prixs.

Fun in the rain, we don't shut when the weather is wet - protective wet weather clothing supplied

We are thrilled to announce our most recent circuit upgrade-------a fully floodlit track. A new exciting after dark experience is up and running by popular demand.

Please call for opening hours and check availability, or visit our website
www.carewkarting.co.uk

103

THE DUNES RIDING CENTRE
Martletwy, Narberth

A visit to Pembrokeshire wouldn't be complete withoutsampling the horse riding at the Dunes Riding Centre. A friendly, family run stables offering riding for all abilities from complete beginners to those wanting a more adventurous ride. Their fit, forward going horses and ponies will take you through woodland and forestry at a pace to suit your ability, ranging from an hour for the experienced, to a half day for the competent rider who can walk, trot and canter. Nervous riders and children can be led on the one hour ride which is suitable for novices from 5 to 75! All prices include the use of approved riding hats and jodphur boots, and it is essential to book in advance. All rides are accompanied by cheerful competent escorts who will make this an experience to remember and cherish.

for more information or to book a visit
tel: 01834 891398

SAILING

Traditionally, dinghy sailing is very popular all over Pembrokeshire and southwest Wales. Yacht clubs such as Newport, Fishguard and Solva in the north of the county and Tenby and Saundersfoot in the South, offer a friendly club atmosphere and a variety of facilities and racing pro-grammes. Along the Milford Haven waterway, perhaps the most popular sailing location because it is sheltered from the open sea, you will find some of the larger and more active clubs, such as Neyland, Pembroke Haven Pembrokeshire (Gelliswick, Milford Haven) and Dale. For yachtsmen, the Haven has 22 miles of navigable inland waterway, with the additional challenge of exciting offshore to the nearby islands of Skomer, Skokholm and Grassholm. There are marinas at Milford Haven and Neyland, pontoons at Dale, Angle, Burton and Neyland and various mooring sites all along the waterway.

DALE YACHT CLUB
tel: 01646 636362

MILFORD MARINA
tel: 01646 696 312

NEYLAND MARINA
tel: 01646 601601

PEMBROKESHIRE YACHT CLUB
Gelliswick,
Milford Haven
tel:01646 692799

Saundersfoot

Solva

PEMBROKESHIRE CRUISING
Neyland Marina,
Brunel Quay, Neyland
tel: 01646 602500

PEMBROKESHIRE WATERSPORTS
Ahoy Pembrokeshire,
15 Church Road,
Hazelbeach,
Milford Haven
SA73 1EB
tel: 0845 427 5608
or
Mobile: 07791 905 954

SOLVA SAILBOATS
1, Maes-y-Forwen
Solva, Haverfordwest
SA62 6TR
tel: 01437 720972

WEST WALES WIND, SURF &SAILING
Dale Sailing Company,
Brunel Quay, Neyland,
Milford Haven, SA73 1PY
tel: 01646 636642

SURFING AND WINDSURFING

Big waves, clear blue unpolluted waters, no crowds and relatively mild air and water temperatures - the tempting combination which Pembrokshire offers to surfers who are willing to travel that bit further in order to stand out from the rest. Late summer and early autumn are particularly good times to take advantage of the county's superb beaches and surfing conditions. Freshwater West, in South Pembrokeshire boasts the biggest and most consistent waves in the whole of Wales, with a variety of breaks to choose from. However there are strong currents and no lifeguards, so beginners should not surf here. Other beaches worth checking out nearby include Broad Haven (south), Freshwater East and Manorbier. In North Pembrokeshire, good surfing can be enjoyed at Whitesands Bay, Newgale, Broad Haven and West Dale. Age is no barrier to windsurfing which attracts enthusiasts from 8 to 80. Some enjoy setting sail in light winds for a tranquil afternoon cruise, whilst others like to display their competitive streak by racing, and for the most adventurous there are the strong winds and wave jumping.

Another big attraction of windsurfing is that it's easy to learn, provided you have the right equipment and and tuition. One of Britain's top windsurfing and sailing venues is Dale. Its mile wide bay promises superb sea sailing on flat water, with no strong tidal currents, and is ideal for beginners and experts alike. West Wales Windsurfing, Sailing and Canoeing, is based on Dale waterfront and is a specialist watersports centre approved by the Royal Yachting Association. The expert tuition available here caters for everyone, from beginner to advanced windsurfers. All equipment is provided including wet-suits and buoyancy aids, and every instructor holds a nationally recognised qualification. As for recommending the best beaches, Broad Haven, (St. Brides Bay) and Newgale are ideal for more experienced windsurfers, except in particularly calm conditions, where as beginners and intermediates will breeze along more easily at Tenby, Saundersfoot, Newport and Fishguard.

SURF SHOPS AND HIRE

HAVEN SPORTS
Broad Haven
tel: 01437 781354

MA SIME'S SURF HUT
St. Davids
tel: 01437 720433

NEWSURF
Newgale
tel: 01437 721398

**TYF
ADVENTURE**
St. Davids
tel: 01437 721611

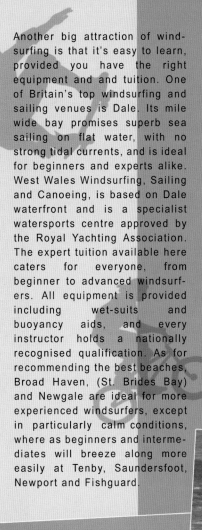

CYCLING ROUTES

Pembrokeshire is the perfect county to see from the comfort of a bicycle. Long flat coastal roads, fantastic scenery and views to be enjoyed at a slow and relaxed pace.

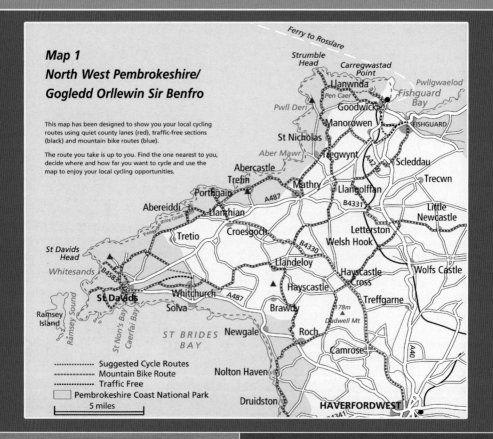

Map 1

North West Pembrokeshire/
Gogledd Orllewin Sir Benfro

This map has been designed to show you your local cycling routes using quiet county lanes (red), traffic-free sections (black) and mountain bike routes (blue).

The route you take is up to you. Find the one nearest to you, decide where and how far you want to cycle and use the map to enjoy your local cycling opportunities.

Ferry to Rosslare

Strumble Head
Carregwastad Point
Pwllgwaelod
Llanwnda
Pen Caer
Fishguard Bay
Pwll Deri
Goodwick
FISHGUARD
Manorowen
St Nicholas
Scleddau
Aber Mawr
Llegwynt
Trecwn
Abercastle
Mathry
Llangolffan
Trefin
Little Newcastle
Porthgain
A487
B4331
Abereiddi
Llanrhian
Letterston
Welsh Hook
Tretio
Croesgoch
B4330
St Davids Head
Wolfs Castle
Whitesands
B4583
Llandeloy
Hayscastle Cross
St Davids
Whitchurch
A487
Hayscastle
Treffgarne
Ramsey Island
Solva
Brawdy
78m
Dudwell Mt
Ramsey Sound
St Non's Bay
Caerfai Bay
ST BRIDES BAY
Newgale
Roch
A40
Camrose
Nolton Haven
A4341
Druidston
HAVERFORDWEST

- - - - - - Suggested Cycle Routes
- - - - - - Mountain Bike Route
- - - - - - Traffic Free
☐ Pembrokeshire Coast National Park
5 miles

CYCLING INFORMATION
www.cyclepembrokeshire.com
www.sustrans.org.uk
www.cycle-n-sleep.co.uk
www.hiddentrails.com

CYCLING ROUTES

Pembrokeshire is the perfect county to see from the comfort of a bicycle. Long flat coastal roads, fantastic scenery and views to be enjoyed at a slow and relaxed pace.

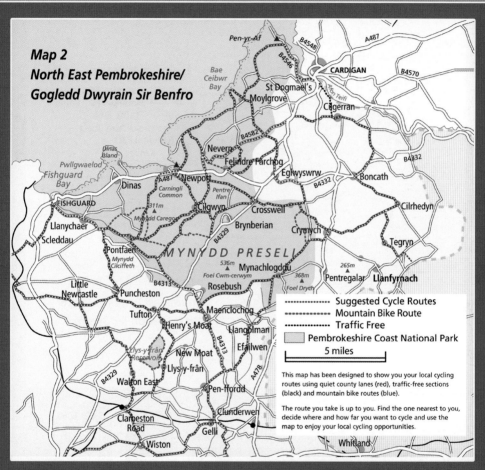

Map 2
North East Pembrokeshire/
Gogledd Dwyrain Sir Benfro

- ················ Suggested Cycle Routes
- ················ Mountain Bike Route
- ················ Traffic Free
- Pembrokeshire Coast National Park

5 miles

This map has been designed to show you your local cycling routes using quiet county lanes (red), traffic-free sections (black) and mountain bike routes (blue).

The route you take is up to you. Find the one nearest to you, decide where and how far you want to cycle and use the map to enjoy your local cycling opportunities.

CYCLING INFORMATION

www.cycling.visitwales.com
www.pembrokeshireoutdoors.org.uk/cycling
www.pcnpa.org.uk
www.touristnetuk.com/Wa/PEMBS/activities/cycling

109

CYCLING ROUTES

Pembrokeshire is the perfect county to see from the comfort of a bicycle. Long flat coastal roads, fantastic scenery and views to be enjoyed at a slow and relaxed pace.

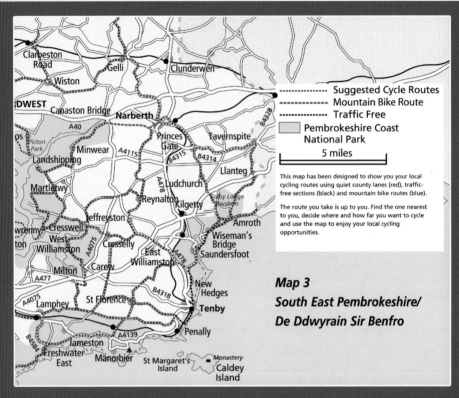

Suggested Cycle Routes
Mountain Bike Route
Traffic Free
Pembrokeshire Coast National Park
5 miles

This map has been designed to show you your local cycling routes using quiet county lanes (red), traffic-free sections (black) and mountain bike routes (blue).

The route you take is up to you. Find the one nearest to you, decide where and how far you want to cycle and use the map to enjoy your local cycling opportunities.

Map 3
South East Pembrokeshire/
De Ddwyrain Sir Benfro

CYCLING ROUTES

Pembrokeshire is the perfect county to see from the comfort of a bicycle. Long flat coastal roads, fantastic scenery and views to be enjoyed at a slow and relaxed pace.

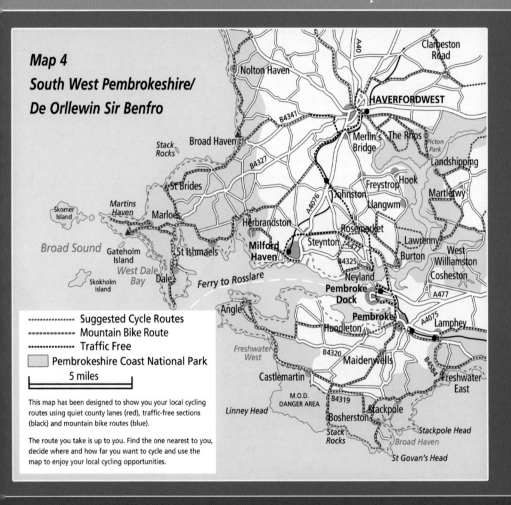

Map 4
South West Pembrokeshire/
De Orllewin Sir Benfro

Legend:
- ·········· Suggested Cycle Routes
- ·········· Mountain Bike Route
- ·········· Traffic Free
- ▢ Pembrokeshire Coast National Park

5 miles

This map has been designed to show you your local cycling routes using quiet county lanes (red), traffic-free sections (black) and mountain bike routes (blue).

The route you take is up to you. Find the one nearest to you, decide where and how far you want to cycle and use the map to enjoy your local cycling opportunities.

Map labels: Clarbeston Road, Nolton Haven, HAVERFORDWEST, Stack Rocks, Broad Haven, Merlin's Bridge, The Rhos, Picton Park, Landshipping, St Brides, Freystrop, Hook, Martletwy, Martins Haven, Skomer Island, Marloes, Johnston, Llangwm, Herbrandston, Rosemarket, Broad Sound, Gateholm Island, St Ishmaels, Milford Haven, Steynton, Lawrenny, Burton, West Williamston, Cosheston, West Dale Bay, Skokholm Island, Dale, Ferry to Rosslare, Neyland, Pembroke Dock, Pembroke, Lamphey, Angle, Hundleton, Freshwater West, B4320, Maidenwells, Castlemartin, M.O.D. DANGER AREA, Linney Head, B4319, Bosherston, Stackpole, Stack Rocks, Broad Haven, Stackpole Head, Freshwater East, St Govan's Head

CYCLING HOLIDAYS

www.greenwayholidays.com
www.mayberryadventures.co.uk/Cycling.php
www.fbmholidays.co.uk/adventure_activities.aspx
www.activitywales.com

THE NORTH COAST

Compared with Tenby and the more developed South, North Pembrokeshire is better known for its rugged beauty and ancient landscape than its leisure attractions and amusements. Yet many of the features which annually bring hundreds of thousands of visitors to the area can be described truthfully as man made - some as long ago as 5000 years. The sights awaiting those visitors with a will to explore are as fascinating as they are varied.

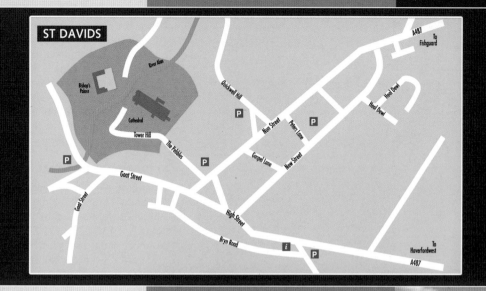

St. Davids is living proof that size is not important. As any visitor will quickly discover, the cathedral city is in reality a modest but very charming village. People still flock here in their thousands as they did throughout the Middle Ages when this was a place of pilgrimage, and the cathedral remains the major object of attention. Yet impressive and hugely significant though it is, the cathedral is small by English standards, and because it is hidden in a sheltered valley you could pass through St. Davids without even noticing that Wales' greatest religious monument is here. The village-cum-city dates back to the 6th century and stands about a mile from the sea, on a wide plateau overlooking the diminutive River Alun. The centre of St. Davids is marked by Cross Square so called because of its restored

ST. DAVIDS

DISTANCES: Fishguard 16m Haverfordwest 16m, Milford Haven 21m, Narberth 25m, Pembroke 26m, Tenby 35m, Carmarthen 46m and London 266m

ancient cross. High Street is something of a misnomer, for the road runs in from Solva and Haverfordwest but does not contain City Hall. Inevitably all roads lead to the 12th century cathedral. Less well known, but no less impressive, are the ruins of the once magnificent Bishop's Palace, which stands opposite the cathedral in Cathedral Close. The close is an area of 18 acres, lying below the city in the vale of the River Alun. It is believed that this secluded site was chosen for the original 6th century church so that it would

Bishops Palace Cross Square

113

THE NORTH COAST

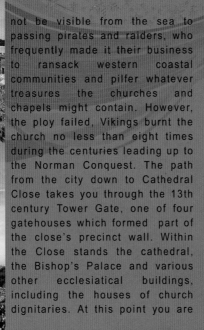

not be visible from the sea to passing pirates and raiders, who frequently made it their business to ransack western coastal communities and pilfer whatever treasures the churches and chapels might contain. However, the ploy failed, Vikings burnt the church no less than eight times during the centuries leading up to the Norman Conquest. The path from the city down to Cathedral Close takes you through the 13th century Tower Gate, one of four gatehouses which formed part of the close's precinct wall. Within the Close stands the cathedral, the Bishop's Palace and various other ecclesiatical buildings, including the houses of church dignitaries. At this point you are still above the level of the cathedral and to reach it requires a further descent of a flight of thirty nine steps known as the Thirty-Nine Articles. The Cathedral and Bishop's Palace are marvels of medieval architecture, all the more striking for the remarkable tranquillity of this remote setting.

ST. DAVIDS CATHEDRAL

The cathedral as it stands today was begun in 1180 by Peter de Leia, the third Norman bishop, and completed in 1522. In 1220 the central tower collapsed, an occurrence apparently not unknown in medieval churches, and further damage was inflicted by a severe earthquake in 1248.

Early in the 14th century, Bishop Gower, nicknamed "The Building Bishop" because of his love of creating great buildings, carried out many changes and improvements to the cathedral. He raised the walls of the aisles, inserted the decorated and much larger windows, built the south porch and transept chapels and vaulted the Lady Chapel. In around 1340 he also built the Bishop's Palace to accommodate the large numbers of pilgrims visiting the cathedral. The Palace, a structure of such spendour that even the ruins are impressive, stands opposite the cathedral. As the cathedral expanded, an increasing number of clerical residences and other ecclesiastical buildings grew up around it, and a wall with gatehouses was built to protect the community. The last of the great builders to contribute to the cathedral was Bishop Vaughan, who in the early 16th century raised the tower to its present height and built the perpendicular chapel dedicated to the Holy Trinity. Following the Reformation the cathedral was

Cross Square St. Davids

115

neglected. The roof was stripped of its lead and subsequently, though much later, collapsed. Severe damage was also inflicted in the Civil War. In 1862 Sir George Gilbert Scott was commissioned to begin a complete restoration of the cathedral, and not surprisingly the work continued into this century. In 1866, during the restoration, the bones of two men were found in a recess which had been walled up. It is believed that these were the remains of St. David and his friend and teacher St. Justinian. They are now contained in an oak chest in the Holy Trinity Chapel. Other tombs in the cathedral include those of Bishop Gower, Edmund Tudor, father of Henry VII, and Giraldus Cambrensis. St. Davids Cathedral which is open to visitors every day, is the largest church in Wales and is certainly the most interesting. The total interior length is nearly 300ft and the tower is 125ft high, small by comparison with cathedrals on the grand scale of York Minster, but a mighty inspiration to the Welsh for centuries past and, no doubt, for centuries to come.

Pembrokeshire Tourist Information Centres
www.visitpembrokeshire.com

SAUNDERSFOOT TIC
The Barbecue
Harbour Car Park
Saundersfoot
SA69 9HE
01834 813672
saundersfoot.tic@pembrokeshire.gov.uk

TENBY TIC
Unit 2
Upper Park Road
Tenby
SA70 7LT
01834 842402
tenby.tic@pembrokeshire.gov.uk

PEMBROKE TIC
Pembroke Library&Information Centre
Commons Road
Pembroke
SA71 4EA
Tel: 01437 776499
Pembroke.tic@pembrokeshire.gov.uk

MILFORD HAVEN TIC
Suite 19
Cedar Court
Havens Head Business Park
SA73 3LS
Tel: 01437 771818
milford.tic@pembrokeshire.gov.uk

HAVERFORDWEST TIC
19 Old Bridge
Haverfordwest
SA61 2EZ
01437 763110
haverfordwest.tic@pembrokeshire.gov.uk

FISHGUARD HARBOUR TIC
Ocean Lab
The Parrog
Goodwick
SA64 0DE
01348 874737
fishguardharbour.tic@pembrokeshire.gov.uk

FISHGUARD TIC
The Town Hall
Market Square
Fishguard
SA65 9HE
01437 776636
fishguard.tic@pembrokeshire.gov.uk

PEMBROKESHIRE COAST NATIONAL PARK VISITOR CENTRES
www.pembrokeshirecoast.org.uk

ORIEL Y PARC
St Davids
SA62 6NW
01437 720392
orielyparc@pembrokeshirecoast.org.uk

NEWPORT TIC
2 Bank Cottages
Long Street
Newport
01239 820912

ST. DAVIDS
CATHEDRAL FESTIVAL

The St Davids Cathedral Festival has been responsible for bringing classical music to the heart of West Wales for the past 32 years. With appearances from some of the finest musical artists in the UK, the festival has built up a reputation as one of the greatest classical music festivals in Wales. Founded in 1979, the St Davids Cathedral Festival is an annual musical event and always takes place during the spring bank holiday, hosting a week of classical and contemporary music concerts set in the stunning surroundings of St. Davids Cathedral, the National Shrine of Wales. The Festival aims to offer as wide a variety of music to as many people as possible. It offers top-class professional concerts at reasonable prices, with free admission for children under 16 at most concerts, and concessions for students, the disabled and unwaged. The style of the concerts is extremely varied; in addition to both early and late evening concerts, (soloists, chamber music ensembles, choral, jazz and orchestral groups) there are also a series of afternoon recitals in which young musicians are offered a platform. The festival also has an established educational outreach programme which also gives local school children the opportunity to perform in the festival. St Davids Cathedral has always had a long tradition of musical excellence. It is remarkable that Britain's smallest city with a population of less than 1,700 and no choir-school, has three outstanding cathedral choirs. The Cathedral Choir is unique in the UK in that it's top line consists of girls, aged 8-18. The choral services of the cathedral form part of the Festival celebrations. The Festival has a strong reputation for excellence and has made a substantial contribution to the cultural life of West Wales. It attracts a considerable number of visitors to the area, many of whom return to the Festival on an annual basis. The Festival provides an excellent opportunity to experience the beautiful Pembrokeshire Coast National Park by day, with music making in the evening by some of the world's top musicians in one of the most historic and revered buildings in Wales.

For further details, or if you wish your name to be added to the mailing list, please contact the Festival Administrator, Katherine Pearce at cathedralfestival@onetel.com or telephone 01437 720057.

ST DAVIDS CATHEDRAL FESTIVAL
GŴYL EGLWYS GADEIRIOL TYDDEWI

27 May – 5 June 2011

Jan Garbarek
Sir Willard White
Natalie Clein
Alexander L'Estrange
Hilliard Ensemble
Carducci String Quartet
Red Priest
BBC National Orchestra of Wales
St Davids Cathedral Choir
St Davids Cathedral Festival Chorus and Orchestra
Alexander Mason
Festival Commission by Francis Grier

Coffee, Lunchtime &
Teatime recitals
Festival Exhibitions

Royal Patron: Her Majesty the Queen.
Brochure available 1st March.
Further details from www.stdavidscathedral.org.uk
Tel: 01437 720057
email:cathedralfestival@onetel.com
Supported by the National Lottery through the Arts Council of Wales

ST. NON'S CHAPEL

Non was the mother of David, the man destined to become the patron saint of Wales. Standing in a field above St. Non's Bay, just south of St. Davids, the original ruined chapel is reputedly the oldest Christian monument in Wales. It is also said to mark the exact spot where St. David was born in the 6th century, during a thunderstorm. Near the chapel is a holy well that miraculously appeared at the moment of birth. In the Middle Ages the well attracted many people who came to cure their ailments. The present St. Non's Chapel was built in 1934.

ST. JUSTINIAN'S

The name actually refers to the remains of St. Justinian's Chapel, but over time it has become synonymous with the little creek and harbour of Porthstinian. The presence of the chapel recalls the legend of St. Justinian, who founded a small religious community on nearby Ramsey Island. The discipline he imposed on his followers was so strict that they rebelled and cut off his head, whereupon St. Justinian picked it up, walked over the sea to the mainland, laid down on his head and died.

PORTHCLAIS

In centuries past, this pictur-esque inlet was a busy little harbour, the port of the monastic community at St. Davids. Its sheltered anchorage saw the comings and goings of countless monks, priests, pilgrims, Norman soldiers, pirates and even Kings. Purple stone from nearby Caerfai and Caerbwdy was landed here to help build the cathedral, along with Irish oak for the roof of the nave. Trade thrived here in the Tudor and Stuart periods, with exports of cereal to the West Country.

Porthclais

PORTHSTINIAN

Porthstinian is well known as the home of the St. Davids lifeboat station. This was founded in 1868, though it was 1912 before the building and slipway were built. The rocky coastline and dangerous offshore reefs, such as the Smalls and the Bishops and Clerks, make this an extremely treacherous area for seaborne traffic, and the life-boats which have seen service here have been involved in many dramatic rescues.

Porthstinian

NORTH COAST SHOPPING

SOLVA

WINDOW ON
WALES
Main St
Solva
Tel: 01437 720659

BAY VIEW STORES
AND POST OFFICE
Tel: 01437 729036

ST DAVIDS

ST DAVIDS FOOD
AND WINE
High Street
Tel: 01437 721948

WINDOW ON
WALES
Cross Square
Tel: 01437 721492

CHAPEL
CHOCOLATES
The Pebbles
Tel: 01437 720023

ST DAVIDS
BOOKSHOP
5a The Pebbles
Tel: 01437 720480

ST DAVIDS
CATHEDRAL
CATHEDRAL SHOP
01437 720060
Domus
01437 720199

BELMONT HOUSE
Cross Square
Tel: 01437 720264

St Davids Post
Office
13 New St
Tel: 01437 720283

FISHGUARD

ORIEL GLAN Y MOR
GALLERY
West Street
Tel: 01348 874787

GWAUN GIFT SHOP
9 West Street
Tel:01348 872224

TENBY HOUSE
40 West Street
Tel: 01348 873898

FISHGUARD POST
OFFICE
57 West Street
Tel: 01348 873863

NATURALS
43 West Street
Tel: 01348 872282

GOODWICK POST
OFFICE
Main Street
Tel: 01348 872842

GWALIA GIFT SHOP
East Street
Tel: 01239 820809

ANGEL HOUSE
NEWSAGENTS
Long Street
Tel: 01239 820640

www.solva.net
www.stdavidscathedral.org.uk
www.stdavids.co.uk
www.newport-pembs.co.uk
www.fishguardonline.com

SOLVA

Without question this must be one of the most charming and attractive coastal villages in Britain. Just east of St. Davids on the A487 Haverfordwest road, Solva is a beautiful rocky inlet which floods at low tide providing a sheltered, safe anchorage for yachts and pleasure craft. Not surprisingly, this fine natural harbour has given the village a long seafaring tradition Shipbuilding and maritime trade flourished here until the railway arrived in Pembrokeshire in the middle of the 19th century. In its heyday the busy port had a thriving import and export business, nine warehouses, twelve limekilns, a direct passenger service to New York and also played an important role in the construction of the two remote lighthouses erected at different times on the smalls, a treacherous cluster of jagged rocks lurking 21 miles off Pembrokeshire's west coast. The facts relating to the passenger service to New York are a particularly fascinating slice of Solva's history. In 1848 the one way fare for an adult was £3. For this you were sure of a bed space, but had to take your own food, and the voyage could take anything from 7 to 17 weeks. The most popular part of this favourite holiday village, which is split into two, is Lower Solva with its harbour, surviving limekilns and a charming selection of shops, pubs and restaurants. Solva is an excellent place to join the Pembrokeshire Coastal Path, as the cliff scenery on either side of the inlet is magnificent. If you fancy an easy stroll you can walk along the harbour or take the footpath above the opposite (eastern) side of the inlet. This takes you to the top of the Gribin - a strip of land between two valleys - where you can see the site of an Iron Age settlement and superb views of the village and harbour.

Solva

Solva

121

MIDDLE MILL

Just north of Solva, a mile up the valley of the river of the same name, nestles the attractive little waterside hamlet of Middle Mill. Here you will find a working woollen mill, which opened in 1907 and has been in production ever since. This family run business invites you to watch the process that turns the finest Welsh wool into a range of high quality rugs, tweeds, carpets and clothes, all of which are for sale on the premises.

Abereiddy

ABEREIDDY

An attractive west facing bay on the north coast of the St. Davids Peninsula, Abereiddy is famous locally for its striking Blue Lagoon once a slate quarry linked to the sea by a narrow channel, but closed in 1904 after it was flooded during a storm. The lagoon is mow considered an important geological feature, and the quarry yields many fossils. The coastal scenery between here and St. Davids Head is outstanding. To the north there are traces of the old narrow gauge railway track which once took the quarried slate and shale to the harbour at nearby Porthgain for export. Abereiddy is about two miles east of Croesgoch, on the A487 St. Davids to Fishguard road.

The Blue Lagoon

PEMBROKESHIRE SHEEPDOGS

On the beautiful north coast of Pembrokeshire, close to St. Davids is Tremynydd Fach Farm, home of Pembrokeshire Sheepdogs Training Centre. The centre runs courses for owners, handlers and their dogs from novice right up to "One Man and His Dog" standard. However, for the casual visitor they also run demonstrations throughout the season, which allow everyone to watch a wonderful exhibition of the skills of the working dogs. From the youngest pups just beginning to show the natural instincts for their work, through all stages of training, to dogs of three or four years at the height of their skills. All can be seen working sheep, and other animals, and clearly having a great time doing it. There is also a surprise finale. Teas and home baked cakes at extremely reasonable prices, plus the opportunity to talk to the handlers, make this a wonderful insight into working dogs. You can even bring your own dog to watch but keep them on a lead please.

**for further information
call 01437 721677**

Abereiddy

THE SLOOP INN *1743 AD*

Porthgain ~ on the Pembrokeshire Coastal Path
Bookings taken for Sunday Lunches and Eveving Meals.

The Sloop Inn, probably the best known pub in the county, is situated just 100 yards from the harbour of Porthgain. Relics and old photographs adorn the walls and ceilings, which makes it as much a museum as a pub. The menu is varied, catering for all tastes including vegetarians and children. A full menu is available 12.00 - 2.30 & 6.00 - 9.30 every day including specials, Sunday Lunches, plus limited choice in the afternoon high season.

The Sloop Inn overlooks the village green where the kids can play and there is reasonably sufficient parking.

Tel: 01348 831449
www.sloop.co.uk

LLANRHIAN

Llanrhian is a hamlet standing at a crossroads on the road between Croesgoch and Porthgain. It is notable because of the unusual parish church, dedicated to St. Rhian, which is cruciform in shape, and has a number of interesting features including a 15th century ten sided font. Also striking is the tall tower, built in the 13th century. The rest of the church was completely rebuilt in 1836 and restored in 1891.

PORTHGAIN

A small hamlet in the parish of Llanrhian, Porthgain is one of the most individual places in Pembrokeshire, with superb coastal scenery and an unpretentious mixture of traditional, Victorian and later style houses and a man made 19th century harbour. The harbour was once a hive of activity and its reconstruction between 1902 and 1904 to make way for larger quays reflected its significant shipping activities. These included the exportation of slate and shale from the quarry at Abereiddy and bricks made from local clay, mainly for local use. The main export however was the medium to fine granite stone; exceptionally hard and used for the construction of buildings and roads as far apart as Liverpool, Dublin and London.

Porthgain

Porthgain was a village whose employment was entirely dependant on the prosperity of the quarry and by the turn of the century, the company known as Porthgain Village Industries Ltd. boasted a fleet of nearly 100 vessels including six steam coasters of 350 tons each. Even as late as 1931, the harbour was improved for a hoped for 170ft 650 ton ship to enter, but after the First World War this maritime trade went into decline and by 1931 had ceased production entirely. In 1983 the Pembrokeshire Coast National Park Authority acquired the attractive harbour and the remains of the buildings bear testimony to Porthgain's industrial past. Porthgain remains a very lively community with a flourishing tourism trade due to its magnificent stretch of coastline and many significant anti quarian remains, making it a must see for those interested in either industrial archaeology or ancient history. A couple of miles north east of Porthgain lies a fine Iron Age fort called Castell Coch. Porthgain is well worth a visit for its diversity of interest. One of Britain's finest geographers described the coast between Porthgain and Abereiddy as the finest in Britain. Today fish are still regularly landed at Porthgain harbour. The Sloop Inn at Porthgain is probably one of the best known pubs in the area. The pub dates back to 1743, when it was more a workers than walkers pub. Nowadays, the Sloop makes a welcome stop for those walking along the coastal path. The premises offer good parking and space for children to play together with a large picnic area.

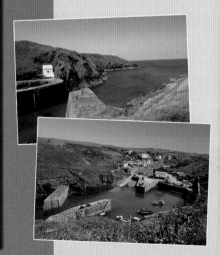

Trefin

Trefin

MATHRY

TREFIN

The village of Mathry stands on a hill just off the A487 between St. Davids and Fishguard, a few miles east of Trefin. Its elevated position gives superb coastal views and of particular interest here is the parish church. This unusual squat building and circular churchyard occupy a prehistoric site, possibly dating from the Iron Age. At one time the church had a steeple that served as a landmark for mariners. Like Trefin, the village is a popular watering hole for visitors passing through. Just west of Mathry is the ancient site of a burial chamber.

Just to the east of Porthgain and its attractive harbour, Trefin is the largest coastal village between St. Davids and Fishguard. It is close to a shingle and sand beach known as Aber Felin and the proximity of the coast path makes this a popular watering hole for walkers. It is worth noting that disabled visitors can gain easy access to this section of the coast path. There is also a youth hostel in the village. Near the shoreline stands the ruin of Trefin Mill, which closed in 1918 and has been partly restored by the National Park Authority. The mill was immortalised in the famous Welsh poem, Melin Trefin.

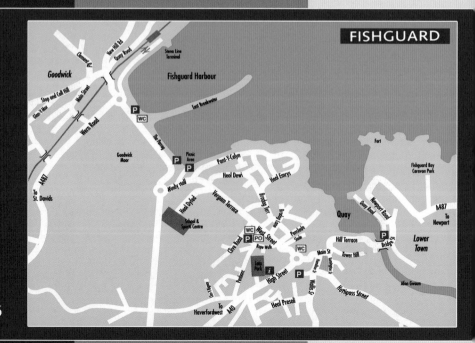

Goodwick

ABERCASTLE

Abercastle stands on Pembrokeshire's rocky northern coastline, southwest of Strumble Head and close to the villages of Trefin and Mathry. From the 16th century onwards this was a busy little coastal port, at various times in its history involved in the export of corn, butter and oats and the import of general goods, anthracite, culm and limestone. The limekiln still survives on the attractive harbour. Abercastle can claim a small piece of important maritime history; in 1876 the first man to sail solo across the Atlantic landed here. Half a mile west of the village, standing just off the coast path, is Carreg Samson, an excellent example of a Bronze Age burial chamber. The capstone is 15ft long and 9ft wide, and according to legend Samson placed it in position using only his little finger.

GOODWICK

Until the harbour was completed in 1906, Goodwick was nothing more than a cluster of fisherman cottages. As the new terminus for the main railway line from London, this one time village quickly adopted the status of a major ferry port and today is still the link between Fishguard and Rosslare in Ireland. Inevitably Goodwick has grown so close, in every sense, to its very near neighbour Fishguard that it is now virtually a suburb of the larger town and the two are synonymous.

FISHGUARD

DISTANCES: Haverforwest 16m, Milford Haven 22m, Narberth 24m, Pembroke 26m, Tenby 35m, Carmarthen 46m and London 272m

Fishguard and Goodwick, 16 miles northeast of St. Davids are the only parts of Pembrokeshire's outer coastline which are not within the National Park. The harbour is in fact the main sailing centre of the North Pembrokeshire coast. Before the harbour, Fishguard had established itself as a very busy port, with slate, corn, butter and cured pilchards and herrings representing the main exports. During the 18th century only Haverfordwest was handling a greater volume of trade. Shipbuilding was important too; the shipyard was renowned for its schooners and square-rigged vessels. The harbour and impressive breakwaters on the Goodwick side of the bay were built in 1906 to attract the transatlantic liners away from Liverpool and Southampton. But as was the reality for Milford Haven, Cardigan, New Quay and other hopeful West Wales ports, the big dream did not materialise. However, there was compensation in successfully establishing the ferry links with Ireland - a lasting and positive return on the massive task of constructing the breakwater, which consumed 800 tones of rock along every foot of its half a mile length. Fishguard has remained a major British ferry port with excellent port facilities. However, its biggest contribution to the history books occurred on 22nd February 1797, when the town was the scene of an extraordinary invasion which has the distinction of being the last invasion on British soil. The uninvited guests were members of a French expeditionary force under the command of an American-Irish adventurer, Colonel William Tate, who had a commission in the French army. His mission was to seize Bristol, at the time Britain's second city, but bad weather forced the ships to land at Carreg Wastad Point, northwest of Fishguard. Once ashore, Tate's troops set about pilfering farms and homesteads, gorging themselves with as much food as they could lay their hands on, washed down with barrels of spirits which local people

The Marine walk, Fishguard

Fishguard

127

had salvaged from a recent shipwreck. In this somewhat unfit condition the soldiers approached the town and, according to local tradition, mistook a crowd of women in red shawls and tall hats for guardsmen. The leader of these women, Jemima Nicholas, a local cobblerwoman, is said to have captured a dozen Frenchmen single handed, armed with only a pitchfork. Her heroism is remembered in the form of a monument in the churchyard at

Lower Town Fishguard

St. Mary's, where she is buried. Within 48hrs of landing the French had surrendered. The heroism of the women has been painstakingly recorded in a vivid and carefully researched tapestry measuring 30 metres which superbly characterises the event. Fishguard is split into two distinct parts. The busy upper part is much like any small town, with many shops, pubs and places to eat. The Lower Town is much older and very attractive, its pretty cottage clustered around the old harbour, where the River Gwaun reaches the sea. In 1971 Lower Fishguard temporarily changed its identity to the fictional town of Llareggub when this pictur esque location was chosen for the the film version of Dylan Thomas's famous radio play "Under Milk Wood", and was also the location for the making of the Orson Welles classic "Moby Dick". The landscape around Fishguard is truly mag-nificent. To the northwest is the dramatic Stumble Head, where the lighthouse is linked to the cliff by a causeway. Dinas Head dominates the coast to the northeast, while inland is the beautiful wooded Gwaun Valley. The whole area is dotted with prehistoric sites.

Visit our exhibition at

OceanLab

Visit our featured exhibition on sea shore life complemented by a number of hands-on displays and activities, and beach explorer.

School Groups and coach parties welcome.

Contact the centre for details of our education pack.

Ocean Lab, The Parrog, Goodwick,
Pembrokeshire, SA64 0DE
Telephone 01348 874737
Fax 01348 872528
Email fishguardharbour.tic@pembrokeshire.gov.uk

Opening times:
Daily, Easter - October 9.30am - 5pm (school summer holidays 9.30am - 6pm)
Daily Winter 10am - 4pm

Facilities on site include: Cyber Café, Soft Play area for under 5s and the computer-based games suitable for all the family.

Why not treat the family to a meal at the Ocean Lab Coffee Shop?

Our information centres offer a local and national accommodation booking service.

Information on places to visit, things to do, walking and cycling routes.

OceanLab

Cymru
Wales

www.pembrokeshireinformationcentres.co.uk

OCEAN LAB
Goodwick, Fishguard

This Information Centre is combined with a cyber café, soft play area, and exhibition. You can explore the ocean and sea using hands on displays and activities as well as fun and informative workbooks. The centre also has a café and a gift shop selling maps, guides, books and souvenirs. Surrounded by the history and heritage of Fishguard and the harbour this centre brings a modern feel to the information service.

The centre is located on the Parrog on the approaches to the ferry terminal at Goodwick.

Opening Times
Easter - October open every day 9.30am - 5pm (open 9. 30am - 6pm school summer holidays)
Daily winter 10am - 4pm

Tel: (01348) 874737
Fax: (01348) 872528
Ocean Lab
Goodwick
Fishguard
SA64 0DE

THE GWAUN VALLEY

The Gwuan Valley is exceptionally beautiful and runs inland from Lower Fishguard to its source high on the slopes of Foel Eryr in the Preseli Hills. It is one of several inland areas of Pembrokeshire which fall within the National Park, and is regarded by geologists as the best example in the British Isles, if not the world, of a sub-glacial meltwater channel. What this means is that about 200,000 years ago, towards the end off one of several recurring Ice Ages which have gripped the planet, the climate became progressively warmer and water began to tunnel beneath the melting ice. This meltwater was under intense pressure, the ice acting as a sort of geological pipe and moved with such tremendous force that it flowed uphill for long stretches. As this unstoppable water eventually crashed into the sea, taking with it huge bolders and blocks of ice, it created deep, steep sided gorges in the landscape. Such are the awesome forces of nature which have given us the spectacular Gwaun Valley. The valley is narrow and sheltered, with heavily wooded sides stretching up to 200ft high. It is rich in wildlife and prehistoric remains, with an abundance of wild flowers and such birds as the buzzard, kestrel, owl, kingfisher, warbler and dipper. The river Gwaun, low and gentle in the summer, becomes a roaring torrent in winter as it rushes down from the Preseli Hills rising behind the valley. Most of the valley's small communities are centred around the hamlets of Llanychaer and Pontfaen. These are largely farming communities, as much of the valley floor is farmed and several farmhouses boast interesting architectural features such as distinctive Flemish style chimneys. The people of the valley are distinctive too, not in appearance, but in the fact that they are sticklers for local tradition. They still celebrate New Years Day on the 13th January according to the old Gregorian calendar - despite the fact that the change to the Julian calendar was made legal in 1752. Other interesting stones can be seen at the restored church in picturesque Pontfaen, where memorial stones dating from the 9th century stand in the churchyard. The ancient woodland of the Gwaun Valley is very precious, and parts of it have been designated as SSSI's (Sites of Special Scientific Interest). The species to be found here include oak, ash, sycamore, alder, blackthorn, hazel, hornbeam,

wild cherry and wych elm. The National Park Authority has established the Cilrhedyn Woodland Centre to promote good woodland management in the valley. Though very much a working centre for the Park Authority's woodland experts and rangers, it is planned to encourage visitors to the centre on a limited number of special open days during the main holiday season. More details of this can be obtained from any National Park Centre. The Golden Road Path takes you from Lower Fishguard to Crymych via the ridge of the Preseli Hills, passing such fascinating features as Bronze Age burial mounds, a Neolithic burial chamber, a particularly fine example of an Iron Age fort and Carn Meini - the source of the bluestone which thousands of years ago mysteriously found its way to Stonehenge for the construction of the monument's inner circle.

Newport

NEWPORT

The town of Newport is a very popular resort. The charming little town sits on the lower slopes of the Carn Ingli, which rises to more than 1100ft above sea level, and the superb stretch of sands on the east side of the Nevern estuary is rivalled only by Whitesands Bay as the best beach in North Pembrokeshire. On the opposite shore of the estuary mouth is Parrog. It was here that Newport developed as a thriving port engaged in fishing, coastal trading and shipbuilding. Newport was an important wool centre. However, this industry faltered when an outbreak of plague hit the town during the reign of Elizabeth I and much business was lost to Fishguard. Later in the port's development slates were quarried from local cliffs went by sea to Haverfordwest, Pembroke, Tenby and parts of Ireland. In 1825 maritime trade received a boost when the quay was built, and come the end of the 19th century Newport boasted five warehouses, several limekilns, coal yards and a shipyard. Today the estuary is silted up and pleasure craft occupy the moorings. As far as the town itself, one of the main features is Newport Castle. This overlooks the estuary and was built in the early 13th century by William FitzMartin. It has had an eventful history: captured by Llywelyn the Great in 1215, then by Llywelyn the Last in 1257, and attacked and damaged in Owain Glyndwr's revolt in 1408, after which it fell into decline. It remained a ruin until 1859, when the gatehouse and one of its towers were converted into a residence. Today the castle is in private ownership and not open to visitors. You can, however, see William FitzMartin's other contribution to Newport. He established St. Mary's, a huge church which is cruciform in plan and features a 13th century Norman tower. Other attractions in Newport include a golf course alongside the sands and the prehistoric cromlech known as Carreg Goetan Arthur, which stands in a field by the bridge. There are many other such sites in the area. On Carn Ingli Common there are prehistoric hut circles and stones and the most famous and striking site of all is Pentre Ifan, 3 miles southeast of Newport.

ANGEL HOUSE
Newport
A long established gift shop and newsagent in the centre of this busy community. Recently refurbished and re-stocked by Ron and Helen, a friendly welcome awaits all visitors. With a range of Welsh and UK made unusual gifts, including gemstone & silver jewellery, quality glassware and ceramics, local-scene greeting cards, toys, beachware, walking guides & maps. On a practical level, there is a watch battery fitting service, photocopying, laminating and fax service. The shelves of old-fashioned 'sweetie-jars' and delicious home-made cakes make Angel House a shop for 'all occasions', popular with locals and visitors alike.

Find us off the A487 on Long Street towards the public car park.

The Royal Oak
NEWPORT CURRY HOUSE
West Street, Newport, Pembrokeshire SA42 0TA

The Royal Oak offers you a warm welcome and good facilities. The front door leads straight into a comfortable lounge bar where you can enjoy a bar meal, or relax with a drink before proceeding upstairs to the restaurant.

Established as the "Curry House" of Newport, we also specialise in fresh fish and grills using local produce wherever possible. Vegetarians and all special diets are catered for and traditional Sunday lunch all year round. Choose your wine from a tempting selection in our wine list. Bar meals are served in the public bar which is fully stocked with a range of real ales, beers and lagers.

Altogether we cater for a wide variety of tastes!

Children Welcome • Popular Traditional Sunday Lunch • Take Away
Food Service • Parties Catered For • Food Served All Day
Large Car Park At Rear • Regret No Dogs Allowed

We operate a No Smoking policy

Open daily all year 11am to 12pm, Sundays 12 to 11.30pm

Tel: 01239 820632

DINAS CROSS

Dinas Cross and its surrounding area is notable for its prehistoric monuments, especially the Bronze Age cairns. Cairns and barrows - mounds of earth or stone and earth - were built throughout the Bronze Age (2000 - 600BC) and often mark the sites of burials. Stone cists at the centre of the mound often contain cremations and pottery vessels and it is thought that the cairns themselves acted as burial sites. The stones for the first stone phase of Stonehenge came from Carn Meini, high in the Preselis. The whole area is littered with prehistoric sites including Iron Age hillforts (600BC - 43AD) and earlier cairns and standing stones. Sites like the spectacular hillfort at the summit of Carningli were clearly used over a long period of time and must have been important spiritual or religious places. Mynydd Melyn, a short distance southeast of Dinas Mountain, contains abundant evidence of prehistoric activity including hut circles (the foundations of pre-historic dwellings) parts of a field system and several cairns.

THE TEIFI ESTUARY

The River Teifi is a natural boundary that lies between Pembrokeshire and Ceredigion and its wide estuary is of great interest. The large and popular beach of Poppit Sands is backed by extensive dunes and has good visitor facilities. The area is also excellent walking and watersports country, and the estuary is a favourite haunt for birdwatchers. The many species to be observed here include gulls, oystercatchers curlews, cormorants and shelduck. The Teifi is also well known for its salmon and sea trout and the ancient Teifi coracle was used by fishermen long before the Romans arrived. The valley of the Teifi, which is a little further inland separates the counties of Ceredigion and Carmarthenshire, is said to be one of the most beautiful river valleys in Britain. It is certainly very scenic, with several picturesque towns and villages along its banks and for visitors to North Pembrokeshire is well worth exploring.

CILGERRAN

Famous for its superb Norman castle, which is perched above the wooded gorge of the Teifi, Cilgerran is a few miles east of Cardigan and was once a slate quarrymens village. It is the venue for the annual coracle regatta, which takes place in August.

Poppit Sands

Teifi Estuary

135

NEVERN

Nevern is an ancient parish on the River Nyfer, close to Newport. Its imposing Norman church, dedicated to the Celtic saint Brynach, has a definite mystique and atmosphere that is compounded by the famous bleeding yew in the churchyard, a broken branch that constantly drips blood red sap. The church features a magnificent 11th century wheel, headed Celtic cross. Above the church, topping a deep ravine, is Nevern Castle, a motte and baily earthwork.

MOYLEGROVE

This attractive coastal village stands on the Newport to St Dogmael's road, a mile from Ceibwr Bay. It dates back to Norman times and nearby are two burial chambers.

ST. DOGMAELS

Facing Cardigan across the Teifi estuary is the picturesque hillside of the village St Dogmaels. It lies close to Poppit Sands, the most northerly beach in the National Park and also at the northern end of the Pembrokeshire Coastal Path. In St Dogmaels you will find the remains of a 12th century abbey built in 1115 by Benedictine monks from France - as a replacement for an earlier Celtic monastery which had stood on the site until Viking raiders destroyed it in the 10th century. The north and west walls of the nave are still standing.

Nevern

St. Dogmaels

Nevern
Churchyard

The Bleeding Yew

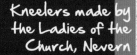

Kneelers made by
the Ladies of the
Church, Nevern

PEMBROKESHIRE EVENTS 2011

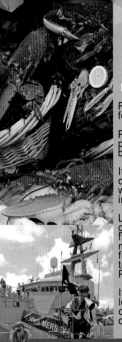

25TH JUNE TO 3RD JULY 2011

MAKE A DATE FOR PEMBROKESHIRE FISH WEEK 2011!

For a small county, it's a whopper of a festival.

Pembrokeshire Fish Week 2011 is packed with more than 250 events between 25th June and 3rd July.

It celebrates the Welsh county's first-class seafood, spectacular coastline, wonderful clean beaches, and fascinating maritime heritage.

Love the outdoors? Come and enjoy guided island and beach walks, eco-fishing adventures, coasteering, and much more. Take an evening boat trip finishing at a riverside pub, or learn how to forage for delicious edibles along the Pembrokeshire coast.

If you're bringing the family, there's loads of fun in store. Explore crystal-clear rockpools and find out what lives on our beaches in seashore safaris.

Learn to windsurf, take part in seaside sports, or make some wonderful creations in beach-inspired art and craft workshops.

And if you love fish and shellfish, then you're in for a treat!

Tuck into the freshest local produce at the county's restaurants and pubs all week long -from local lobster to fresh crab salads and seafood extravaganzas, or good old beer-battered fish with hand-cut Pembrokeshire chips.

There are also lots of opportunities for cooks to learn how to get the best out of their fish and shellfish, with master-classes, workshops and speciality cookery classes.

The festival is also a feast for anglers of all ages and level of ability. Come and pit your wits against the best in sea angling and coarse fishing championships. There are also family coaching days and learn-to-fish sessions if you fancy getting hooked on one of Britain's favourite sports.

Pembrokeshire Fish Week is organised by Pembrokeshire County Council.

The festival won the Gold Award in the Food Tourism Destination category in the True Taste Food and Drink Awards 2009/ 2010, and Pembrokeshire Tourism's 'Premier Event Award' 2009 / 2010.

It is part funded through the Rural Development Plan for Wales 2007-2013, which is financed by the EU and the Welsh Assembly Government.

For more information, view www.pembrokeshirefishweek.co.uk or contact Kate Morgan on: 01437 776168

You can also follow us on twitter and join our facebook group.

Neil and Christine from the True Taste Award-winning Claws Shellfish selling their fresh seafood at Pembrokeshire Fish Week 2010's opening family fun day at Milford Haven Marina.

Expert fish craftsman Duncan Lucas holding a filleting demonstration at Pembrokeshire Fish Week 2010's family fun day at Tenby.

Children enjoying a marine fun day at Stackpole in Pembrokeshire Fish Week 2010

JANUARY

Saundersfoot New Years Day Swim
Jan 1st
www.visit-saundersfoot.com

Whitesands New Years Day Swim
Jan 1st
www.penknifeclub.co.uk

Little Haven New Years Day Swim
Jan 1st

FEBRUARY

St Davids Day Food and Craft
Market – including the cawl cooking
championship of the World and
Elsewhere.
Saundersfoot.
26th Sat – 27th Sun
www.visit-saundersfoot.com

MARCH

St Davids Day Events, St Davids
On and around March 1st

APRIL

Easter Farmers Market
Haverfordwest
Good Friday

West Wales Health Show
Withybush Showground
Haverfordwest
01348 881269

MAY

Fishguard Folk Festival
Spring Bank Holiday
Friday 27th May – Monday 30th May
www.pembrokeshire-folk-music.co.uk

St Davids Cathedral Festival
Fri 27th May – Sunday 5th June
www.stdavidscathedral.org.uk

Pembrokeshire Preseli
Walking Festival
Sunday 1st May – Tues 31st May
information@planed.org.uk
or 01834 860965

JUNE

Pembrokeshire Fish Week, All
over the county
www.pembrokeshire.gov.uk/fishweek

JULY

Tenby Summer Spectacular
(1 of 2), Tenby Harbour

AUGUST

Tenby Summer Spectacular
(2 of 2), Tenby Harbour

Pembrokeshire County Show
Withybush Showground
Haverfordwest
www.pembrokeshirecountyshow.co.uk

SEPTEMBER

The Really Wild Food
Festival, St Davids

Pembrokeshire Classic Car Run
Starts in Haverfordwest
Finishes Tenby.
Sunday 4th September

OCTOBER

Harvest Fayre, Farmers Market,
Haverfordwest
01437 776168

NOVEMBER

Various firework and bonfire displays
On and around Friday 5th November

DECEMBER

St Nicholas Christmas Market,
Saundersfoot
www.visitsaundersfoot.co.uk

Tenby Winter Carnival Festival
www.tenbyevents.co.uk

Tenby Boxing Day Swim,

New Years Eve Celebrations,
Fishguard/Tenby/Saundersfoot
Saturday 31st December

Pembrokeshire PRODUCE

Pembrokeshire Produce
www.pembrokeshire.gov.uk/foodanddrink

The Really Wild Food Festival
www.reallywildfestival.co.uk

Narberth Food Festival
www.narberthfoodfestival.co.uk

Cwm Deri vineyard
www.cwm-deri.co.uk

Yerbeston Gate Farm
www.farmshopfood.co.uk

Pembrokeshire Organic Meat
www.pembrokeshirecoastorganicmeat.co.uk

Whole foods of Newport
www.wholefoodsofnewport.co.uk

Pembrokeshire is rich with local food produce. There are several annual food festivals and award winning local Farmers Markets on alternate Fridays on the Riverside in Haverfordwest, as well as the Farmers Market held in the new Town Hall in Fishguard, found on alternate Saturdays. There is also a daily indoor market in Tenby and fantastic delicatessens through-out the county such as the award winning Andrew Rees situated in Narberth. Why not take a trip to the Cwm Deri Vineyard at Martletwy, or take full advantage of the stunning settings by taking a picnic to the beautiful beaches, glorious cliff-tops or breathtaking islands.

Pembrokeshire
GREEN LIVING

Holidaying here in Pembrokeshire is always an environmentally sound choice. Here are some simple tips for maximising your contribution to the planet that we all share, quick and easy suggestions that can make a big difference.

The energy saving trust
www.energysavingtrust.org.uk

Celtic Bio-diesel
www.celticbiodiesel.co.uk

The slow food movement
www.slowfood.com

Pembrokeshire Produce
www.pembrokeshire.gov.uk/foodanddrink

Pembrokeshire Produce
www.pembrokeshireproducedirect.org.uk

Green Dragon Environmental Awards
www.greendragonems.com

St Davids Eco City
www.eco-city.co.uk

West Wales Eco Centre
www.ecocentre.org.uk

North Pembrokeshire eco-festival
www.northpembsenergy.org.uk

Fair Trade
www.fairtrade.org.uk

Alternate Technology
www.alternativetechnology.org.uk

Top Tips

Actively seek out accommodation bearing the "Green Dragon" Environmental Award

Walking or Cycling are great ways to slow your pace and enjoy the county

Take advantage of local transport such as the Coastal Buses, see page 175

If you are driving around the county, cut down wind resistance by removing roof racks and other accessories if you're not using them: a fully loaded roof rack increases consumption by 30%

Source out locally produced foods, try farmers markets and farm shops

When dining out look for Pembrokeshire Produce labels

Milford Haven and Haverfordwest have both been designated as Fair Trade towns

INLAND PEMBROKESHIRE

In the ancient Welsh tales of The Mabinogion, Pembrokeshire was described as "Gwlad hud a lledrith" - the land of magic and enchantment. Nowhere is this more evident than in the wild , mysterious Preseli Hills. These rolling moorlands, often overlooked by visitors on their way to the coast, are the major upland region of the National Park, presenting a stark contrast to the relatively flat coastal plateau.   The evidence left by the earliest settlers suggests man has occupied the hills for at least 5000 years. Neolithic burial chambers, Bronze Age cairns, stone circles, standing stones and Iron Age forts litter this untouched Celtic landscape.

When Neolithic (New Stone Age) farmers arrived in Pembrokeshire, well versed in the art of raising crops and herding animals, they were the first people to work the land here. They fashioned implements such as axes, hammers and hoes from Preseli dolerite (bluestone), and archaeologists believe that two so called axe factories existed on the Preseli Hills, though their sites have never been identified. The dwellings of these distant ancestors were too flimsy to stand up to the ravages of time. But not so their tombs (cromlechau), which are concentrated along the coastal plateau and in the Preseli foothills. Pentre Ifan, on the hills northern slopes, and Carreg Samson, on the coast near Abercastle, are two of the finest prehistoric monuments to be found anywhere in Wales. Later Bronze Age man also left his burial sites on the Preseli Hills, in the form of round cairns. A fine example is to be found on top of Foel Drygarn. There is another on the summit of Foel Cwm Cerwyn, the highest point in all of Pembrokeshire. On exceptionally clear days the views from here are astonishing. You can see west to the Wicklow Mountains of Ireland, north to Snowdonia, east to the Brecon Beacons and south across the Bristol Channel to the counties of the West Country. Another ancient relic adorning the Preseli Hills is the interesting stone circle known as Gors Fawr. This stands on the moorland west of the hamlet of Mynachlogddu. It comprises 16 stones and 2 large outlying pointer stones and its diameter exceeds 70ft. But the biggest mystery of all to emanate from these brooding hills, and one which never seems likely to be answered, concerns the inner circle at Stonehenge, 180 miles from Preseli on Salisbury Plain. Much of this inner circle is made from bluestone, which is dolerite, rhyolite and volcanic ash, found only at Carn Meini on the eastern crests of the Preseli Hills. The mystery is how the 80 stones, weighing up to 4 tonnes each and over 250 tonnes in total, made the incredible journey from Preseli to Salisbury Plain during the third millennium BC. The most likely explanation seems to be that they were taken by boat along rivers up the Bristol Channel, crossing the overland stretches on sledges which had rollers underneath. This would have taken a gargantuan effort by a huge army of labour. Even so, this theory has found much wider acceptance than the two others proposed. One is that the stones were carried to Salisbury Plain by the great Irish Sea Glacier, the biggest flow of glacial ice ever to cover Britain, long before

Pentre Ifan

View over Newport

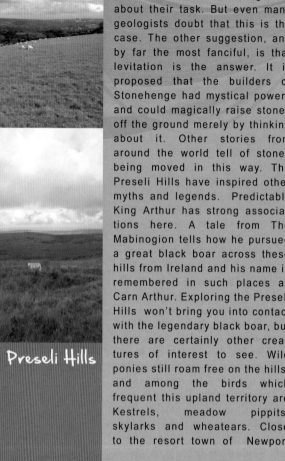

Preseli Hills

the builders of Stonehenge set about their task. But even many geologists doubt that this is the case. The other suggestion, and by far the most fanciful, is that levitation is the answer. It is proposed that the builders of Stonehenge had mystical powers and could magically raise stones off the ground merely by thinking about it. Other stories from around the world tell of stones being moved in this way. The Preseli Hills have inspired other myths and legends. Predictably King Arthur has strong associations here. A tale from The Mabinogion tells how he pursued a great black boar across these hills from Ireland and his name is remembered in such places as Carn Arthur. Exploring the Preseli Hills won't bring you into contact with the legendary black boar, but there are certainly other creatures of interest to see. Wild ponies still roam free on the hills, and among the birds which frequent this upland territory are Kestrels, meadow pippits, skylarks and wheatears. Close to the resort town of Newport

are such delights as Nevern, with its haunting church and the reconstructed Iron Age hillfort at Castell Henllys. A little further north are the dramatic cliffs of Cemaes Head, where the exposed rocks have been folded by the tremen dous forces exerted by movements deep in the earth. The cliffs of the headland are over 500ft high in places, the highest in Pembrokeshire and they look down to the mouth of the Teifi estuary. Like any upland area, the Preseli Hills are best explored on foot, and apart from sheep the most common species you are most likely to encounter in these wilds are hill walkers, Ornithologists, botanists, archaeologists, artists, photographers and others of strange pursuits also seem to find the hills a suitable habitat. However, unless you are familiar with the hills, it is advisable to take a map and compass on your travels. The average rainfall on the hills is nearly twice as much as it is on the coast and the mists have a tendency to come down very suddenly. This is also part of Pembrokeshire where winter snow falls on anything like a regular basis.

Castell Henllys

Nevern

Llys·y·Frân

COUNTRY PARK & RESERVOIR

A visit to Llys-y-Frân Country Park and Reservoir has long been one of Pembrokeshire's favourite days out.

There's such a wide variety to interest the whole family – from a short stroll to a full-stretch walk, from cycling to rowing, or simply enjoying the spectacular views of the 100ft high dam and the surrounding countryside... the list is endless and we're sure you'll want to come back again and again.

For further information about Llys-y-Frân, please ring the Visitor Centre on 01437 532273 or 01437 532694 or fax us on 01437 532732.

Park open 8 am - dusk during the season (9 am in Winter)

WALKING · FISHING · CYCLING · PLAYGROUND · HIRE BOATS · RESTAURANT · GIFT SHOP

An alternative way of exploring the Preseli Hills is to join a guided walk or horse riding lesson which are run by the National Park Authority, as part of its annual activities and events programme. For more information contact any National Park Information Centre.

LLYS-Y-FRAN RESERVOIR & COUNTRY PARK

Close to the picturesque village of Rosebush, beautiful Llys-y-Fran Country Park incorporates the 212 acre reservoir that supplies most of Pembrokeshire's drinking water. Around this man made lake are mature woodlands and open grassland, with superb views of the Preseli Hills and surrounding farmland. In spring the carpets of bluebells in the woods are a sheer delight and throughout the season the country park is vibrant with the colours of countless varieties of wild flowers. In recent years improvements have been made to the park, following a scheme to increase the size of the reservoir. An example of which is the much wider footpath right round the reservoir and the 20, 000 broad leafed trees which have been planted. As a result the six and a half mile perimeter walk is now even more enjoyable than ever. Near the main car park is the children's adventure

149

playground to keep youngsters amused. Mountain bikes are another treat that families can enjoy. Bikes can be hired by the hour or by the day and with the reservoir perimeter path serving as a cycle track, this can be a fun activity in which everyone can participate. Fishing is another leisure pursuit which has always been popular here, and Llys-y-Fran attracts anglers from all over Wales and beyond. Little wonder as few fisheries can match the country park's excellent facilities. These include a purpose built boathouse with a fleet of loch-style petrol engine fishing boats ideal for fly fishermen. During the season over 20,000 top quality rainbow trout are released into the freedom of the lake from their rearing cages. A healthy population of brown trout adds variety to the sport. For watersport enthusiasts the reservoir is perfect both for beginners and for more experienced sailors but you must bring your own craft as no hire is available. The park shop does however offer launching permits for dinghies, sailboards and canoes. As you would expect in a country park of Llys-y-Fran's status and reputation, wildlife is of prime concern in the management of the park. The oak and coniferous woodlands and rough grass provide ideal habitats for a variety of birds. More than 140 species have been recorded

here. Llys-y-Fran licensed restaurant enjoys superb views across the reservoir and countryside and is housed in the Visitor Centre alongside the gift and souvenir shop. The restaurant offers excellent service and opens March to the end of October. It is also worth noting that Llys-y-Fran Country Park has strong historical and musical connections. Near the base of the reservoir dam is a tumble down cottage, the birthplace of the famous Welsh composer William "Penfro" Rowlands. It was in gratitude for his son's recovery from a serious illness that he was inspired to write the tune for Blaenwern, one of the best loved of all hymn tunes. A monument to William Rowlands, erected by Welsh Water now stands near the ruins of the old cottage.

for further information
tel: 01437 532273
or 01437 532694

ROSEBUSH

Rosebush enjoys an unusual if modest claim to fame, slates from its quarries were used to roof the Houses of Parliament. But the village could have become a well known tourist attraction in the 19th century had everything gone according to plan. When the Clunderwen - Maenclochog railway opened in 1876 to serve the quarry there were big ambitions to develop Rosebush as an inland spa. A small tourist industry did develop here, but nothing like on the scale imagined.Rosebush is close to Llys-y-Fran Reservoir and Country Park and stands below the summit of Foel Cwm Cerwyn, in a superb setting which is ideal for walking. In 1992 a visitor centre and museum was opened in the village's old post office.

MYNACHLOGDDU

This small pastoral community of the Preseli Hills once belonged to the monastery at St. Dogmaels. It stands east of Rosebush, close to the impressive Gors Fawr Stone Circle, which is over 70ft in diameter. A commemorative stone to the poet Waldo Williams is also nearby.

NEW MOAT

This small village stands in the Preseli foothills, just east of Llys-y-Fran Country Park. A mound marks the site of a Norman motte and bailey castle. The church, distinctive for its tall tower, has an early 17th century altar tomb.

MAENCLOCHOG

A small Victorian church on the village green is the central feature of this sprawling community on the southern slopes of the Preseli Hills, a couple of miles north east of Llys-y-Fran Country Park. For many years the village has served the needs of the area and early this century Maenclochog boasted a blacksmith, miller, carpenter, lime burner, wheelwright, draper and no fewer than 10 pubs. A mile from the village is Penrhos, the only thatched cottage in the area and is now a museum.

CRYMYCH

Crymych, situated on the A478 Tenby to Cardigan road, is a 19th century hillside village which grew up around the railway. The Whitland Cardigan line was completed in 1880 and no longer exists, but the village has remained an important agri-cultural centre and an ideal base from which to

explore the Preseli Hills. Within easy reach are Foel Drygarn, where cairns and an early Iron Age fort are to be found and the 1300ft summit of Y Frenni Fawr.

BONCATH

Between Crymych and Newcastle Emlyn, Boncath takes its name from the Welsh word for buzzard. A former railway village, it is notable for two houses - Ffynone, designed by John Nash in 1792 and Cilwendeg, a Georgian house built by Morgan Jones.

EGLWYSWRW

A compact little village near Castell Henllys Iron Age fort, north of the Preseli Hills, this place with the unpronounceable name, is where St. Wrw is buried. The pre-Christian churchyard is circular and other interesting historical features include the medieval inn, the remains of a motte and bailey castle and a prehistoric ringwork.

CASTELL HENLLYS
IRON AGE FORT

This remarkable and archaeological important example of an Iron Age fort is managed by the National Park Authority and has been partially reconstructed with thatched roundhouses, animal pens, a smithy and a grain store. Recently the site was the location of the BBC's "Surviving the Iron Age" series. The Visitor Centre houses an exhibition which serves as an introduction to the life of the early Celts in Wales. Castell Henllys probably flourished between the 4th century BC and the 1st century AD, when the Romans began their conquest of Britain. The Iron Age Celts were a fierce and warlike people and many of their chieftains lived in well defended forts, of which Castell Henllys was typical. Sited on a valley spur, it had natural defences on three sides, and where the spur joined the side of the valley massive earthworks were thrown up, topped with timber palisades. Stone walling protected a narrow gateway which can still be seen. Such elaborate defences would have employed a huge labour force and this suggests that Castell Henllys was occupied by a leader of some importance along with family, retainers and even a band of warriors. The introduction to the site of domestic animals which flour- ished in the Iron Age has given a further insight into the daily life of these ancient ancestors. A self guided trail takes you through Castell Henllys with information interpretive panels along the way. This is a wonderful place for schools and study groups and an Education Centre has been built in the valley below

Castell Henllys

Castell Henllys

Castell Henllys

the fort. To further recapture the atmosphere and spirit of this mystical historic site, which stands in beautiful North Pembrokeshire countryside below the summit Carn Ingli, special events are held throughout the holiday season, including shows given by the Prytani, an Iron Age Celtic reenactment group. Castell Henllys, just off the A486 a few miles east of Newport, is open daily from Easter to October.

tel: 01239 891319
www.castellhenllys.com

THE LANDSKER BORDERLANDS

When the Normans invaded Pembroke in 1093 and took the site on which the magnificent castle now stands, they were quick to consolidate their domination of South Pembrokeshire and the lands they had gained here. To the north of the county the rebellious Welsh proved more troublesome. The Norman response was to build a line of castles to protect their newly won territory, effectively dividing north from south.These formidable fortresses stretched from Llanstephan in the southeast to Roch in the northwest. They marked what has become known as the Landsker Line, a word of Norse origin meaning frontier.

Narberth Castle

Originally a military device, the Landsker evolved into a cultural and linguistic divide and its effects are evident even today. For example, in the north of the county Welsh is still spoken and many of the place nanes are Welsh also. Churches are usually small, with bellcotes and no towers. By comparison in the anglicised south, English is the dominant language as is clear from the names of the towns and villages, and the Norman churches are characterised by tall, square towers which served as lookouts. One of the castles of the Landsker Line was Narberth. Its scant ruins still stand near the centre of this important market town, which is 10 miles north of Tenby. Narberth is at the heart of a beautiful and historic part of Inland Pembrokeshire known as the Landsker Borderlands. The Borderlands spill over into old Carmarthenshire and are bounded by the River Taf to the east, the Daugleddau estuary to the west, hills and valleys to the north and vales and plains to the south. As awareness of the Borderlands increases a growing number of visitors are exploring this largely undiscovered area of great rural delights. The attractive countryside of the Landsker Borderlands, rich in heritage and wildlife, is typified in the north by lush farmland sweeping down from the Preseli Hills.

FIRE & ICE

A Delicious Selection Of Locally Produced Ice Creams

12 Fantastic Flavours;

Cointreau & Orange

Sorbets; Lemon, Rasberry **Toffee Fudge** Pistachio

Irish Coffee Strawberry & Cream

Banoffee Pie Turkish Delight Cherry Delight

Mint Choc Chip Mad About Chocolate

Dairy free sorbets, Sugar free & Gluten free avilable.

Take Home Tubs Available (0.75ltr & 1ltr) - Flavours Change Weekly

Opening Times: Monday to Saturday 12pm - 5pm

65, ST JAMES STREET, NARBERTH, PEMBROKESHIRE, SA67 7DB (Near Barclays)

DESIGN BY JAMIEKING.CO.UK

NARBERTH

DISTANCES: Fishguard 24m, Haverfordwest 9m, Milford Haven 14m, Pembroke 15m, St. Davids 25m, Tenby 10m, Carmarthen 21m and London 241m

This delightful little town, with its colour-washed Georgian houses, castle ruins and amazing variety of original shops is an essential visit. In recent years the town has become a centre for artists and craftspeople, many of whose works are sold here. Jewellery, pottery, paintings, fabrics, glassware, clothing and woodworks are all represented. Some of the shops and galleries sell a variety of goods while others specialise in the makers' own work.

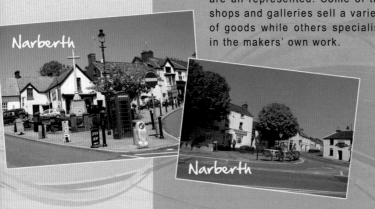

Narberth

Narberth

Narberth Castle

155

INLAND PEMBROKESHIRE

Narberth

This creative movement may be relatively recent but Narberth's history is a long and fascinating one. Standing just south of the Landsker, it falls into the area regarded as "Little England beyond Wales" but its roots lie deep in Welsh history, culture and tradition. The Welsh princes of Dyfed lived here in the dark ages and the town, called by its Welsh name Arberth, features in the ancient stories of the Mabinogion. Narberth castle of which little now remains, was part of the Norman frontier separating north from south. It was captured by the Welsh on numerous occasions and destroyed by Cromwell's forces during the Civil War. Narberth is also remembered for the infamous Rebecca Riots of the 19th century. These began in 1839 with the burning of toll gates in Efailwen, a hamlet in the Preseli foothills a few miles north of the town. This anger was in response to the decision by rich landowners to impose crippling road tolls on the small and impoverished farming communities. The men responsible for torching the toll gates avoided recognition by dressing in women's clothing and blackening their faces, and they addressed their leader as "Rebecca". The dispute quickly became more widespread and other toll gates were destroyed just as quickly as they could be erected. The riots often described as a "true people's revolt" because they had their cause in natural justice, went on for a period of several years. It is one of the ironies of local history that when the authorities called out the troops in a bid to discover the identity of Rebecca and his followers, they were billeted in Narberth's poor-house. Rebecca's Cell can be

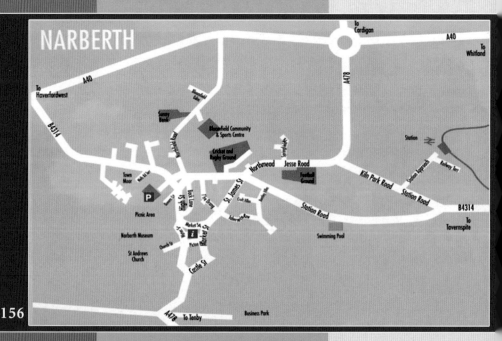

seen under the old Town Hall which now houses a craft shop. Narberth Castle of which little now remains, was part of the Norman frontier separating north from south. It was captured by the Welsh on numerous occasions and destroyed in the Civil War by Cromwell's forces. The castle ruins have been consolidated and are now open to the public all year. Narberth's small but attractive town centre is distinctive for its Town Hall and pleasant Georgian houses. With the promotion of the Landsker Borderlands and other rural areas, Narberth has been revitalised. PLANED (Pembrokeshire Local Action Network for Enterprise and Development) has its headquarters here and the town is very close to a number of the county's most popular attractions such as, Heron's Brook Golf Course, Oakwood, CC2000, Blackpool Mill,Picton Castle, Llawhaden Castle, Holgan Camp Iron Age Hillfort and Folly Farm. These are in addition to those places of interest in Narberth itself, which include a wealth of interesting and unusual shops featuring antiques, art and crafts and galleries as well as many varied and interesting places to eat.

THE QUEENS HALL

A great arts, music and entertainment venue situated in High Street (next to the town's free car park) with a variety of events to suit all tastes. Gallery and cafe.

for more information
tel: 01834 861212

The Creative Cafe

Narberth Town Hall

NARBERTH SHOPPING

AUDREY BULL ANTIQUES
15 High Street
Tel: 01834 861199

THE MALTHOUSE
Back Lane
Tel: 01834 860303

CELTIC VISION
66 ST JAMES ST
NARBERTH. SA67 7DB
Tel: 01834 869123
www.celtic-vision.co.uk
Binoculars, cameras &
camera equipment

ANDREW REES
29 High Street
Tel: 01834 861892

NO 47
47 High Street
Tel: 01834 869110

LIZ'S BAKERY
12 High Street
Tel: 01834 861039

NOBLES
4 High St
Tel: 01834 861135

POST OFFICE
9 High St
Tel: 01834 861337

THE CREATIVE CAFE
Spring Gardens
Tel: 01834 861651

THE WELSH FARMHOUSE COMPANY
35, High Street
Tel: 01834 861123

NEXT DOOR FLORIST
21 High Street
Tel: 01834 861032

FABRIC HOUSE
6 High Street
Tel: 01834 861063

WISEBUYS
18, High Street
Tel: 01834 861880

GOLDEN SHEAF
25 High Street
Tel: 01834 860407

HAULFRYN
13 High Street
Tel: 01834 861902

JELLY EGG
The Old Town Hall
Tel: 01834 860061

ANIMAL KITCHEN BOOKSHOP
Moorfield Terrace
Tel: 01834 860811

www.narberth.co.uk
www.narberthfoodfestival.co.uk
www.thequeenshall.org.uk
www.narberthmuseum.co.uk
www.thenarberthgallery.co.uk
www.pembrokeshire.gov.uk

CLUNDERWEN

Situated just inside Carmathenshire and known until the 1870's as Narbeth Road. The village of Clunderwen developed with the coming of the railway in 1852. An interesting historical anecdote is that it was here in 1913 that the James Brothers first flew their biplane - one of the earliest flights in Wales.

EFAILWEN

Efailwen is recorded in the history books as the place where the erection of a toll gate in 1839 sparked off the Rebecca Riots. Nearby at Glandy Cross is a group of Neolithic and Bronze Age sites, regarded as the most important in South Wales.

LAMPETER VELFREY

There are several prehistoric sites in the immediate area, including tumuli, a Bronze Age hearth and three Neolithic burial chambers.

LLANBOIDY

Llanboidy lies across the border in old Carmarthenshire, about 5 miles north of Whitland, in the small Gronw Valley. A well in the village was the focus of many medieval pilgrimages. Close to Llanboidy are two ancient sites, a cromlech at Cefn Brafle and Arthur's Table, a tumulus, which is in a wood at Dolwilym. Today the village enjoys fame as the home of Pemberton's Victorian Chocolates.

Llawhaden Castle

GELLI

Located just north of Llawhaden, the small community of Gelli developed around a large woollen mill. This worked from the late 19th century until 1937 and was one of several mills which flourished in the Landsker Borderlands at that time. Fishing was another important industry here. In the late 19th century 6 pairs of Cleddau coracles fished here between Gelli and Llawhaden.

LLAWHADEN

Llawhaden was an important medieval settlement standing on the Landsker Line. The original Norman castle was later developed as a magnificent bishops palace by the Bishop's of St. Davids. The ruins which stand today are evidence of the grandeur of this fortified palatial residence. You can also see the remains of a medieval hospice chapel. The Norman church of St. Aidan stands in the valley below, on the banks of the Eastern Cleddau, in a very picturesque position.

LLAWHADEN CASTLE
Originally a wooden structure

built in Norman times, the castle was rebuilt by the Bishops of St. Davids between the late 13th and 15th centuries and transformed into a great fortified palace. This comprised several buildings set around a five sided courtyard, strengthened with angled corners. The ruins now in the care of CADW (Welsh Historic Monuments), include the front of the gatehouse which still stands to its full height, the Great Hall, bakehouse, barracks, visitors' lodgings and the Chapel of the Blessed Virgin. After using the castle for more than 250 years, the bishops dismantled it and stripped the lead from the roof. Close to the castle are two other historic attractions - a restored medieval hospice and Holgan Camp, an Iron Age fort to which visitors now have access thanks to the opening of a new public footpath. The site of the camp was overgrown for centuries until cleared and fenced by PLANED and CADW. Holgan Camp had formidable defences and is a well preserved example of an Iron Age defended enclosure. Many such camps were established in the area.

Llawhaden
Castle
Gatehouse

Llawhaden
Castle

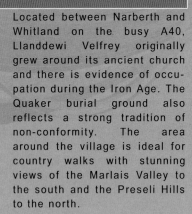

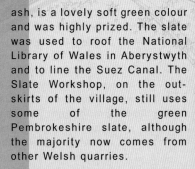

Ludchurch

LLANDDEWI VELFREY

Located between Narberth and Whitland on the busy A40, Llanddewi Velfrey originally grew around its ancient church and there is evidence of occupation during the Iron Age. The Quaker burial ground also reflects a strong tradition of non-conformity. The area around the village is ideal for country walks with stunning views of the Marlais Valley to the south and the Preseli Hills to the north.

LLANDISSILIO

This village stands on the A478 north of Narberth, a road which has developed from a prehistoric route that linked the Preseli Hills and the Cleddau estuary. Castle sites and earthworks suggest that the parish has a long history, an idea supported by the inscribed stones in the church which date back from the 5th or 6th century.

LLANGOLMAN

Robeston
Wathen

From Efailwen, on the A478, the road to Llangolman gives breathtaking views of the approaching Preseli Hills. Until a few years ago, this small village encompassed the last working Pembrokeshire slate quarry Gilfach. The slate, which was formed from volcanic

ash, is a lovely soft green colour and was highly prized. The slate was used to roof the National Library of Wales in Aberystwyth and to line the Suez Canal. The Slate Workshop, on the outskirts of the village, still uses some of the green Pembrokeshire slate, although the majority now comes from other Welsh quarries.

ROBESTON WATHEN

The earliest record of Robeston Wathen dates back as far as 1282. The small hilltop community, on the A40, has a Norman Church and distinctive tower. The part of the parish name Robeston is of Norman origin, whose Kings sought to impose their rule on this part of Wales. The Parish was called at this time Villa Robti or "Robert's Ton" although no records indicate who Robert was. However in the 13th century a family by the name Wathen was granted the titular Lordship of the Manor, and so the village has been named Robeston Wathen ever since. This family had interests in the production and weaving of wool, which was to remain the major export of England and Wales for several centuries. Some indication of the importance of this trade can be seen from

the fact that Geoffrey Chaucer, the author of Canterbury Tales, earned his living as the Kings Wool Talleyman. Today he would have been called a Chief Inspector of Customs and Excise. The Wathen family moved to the Cotswolds, Gloucester and Bristol in Elizabethan times - then great centres of the wool trade. The Wathen family have served with distinction in Church, State and banking. One John de Wathen became Bishop of Salisbury and his 14th century tomb can be seen in Westminster Abbey.

REYNALTON

Reynalton, situated west of Begelly and south of Narberth, is now a small, quiet hamlet in the midst of farmland. Yet earlier in the century coal mining was a thriving local industry, as the village stands in the old South Pembrokeshire coalfield.

TAVERNSPITE

Tavernspite is on the Pembs/Carms border at the junction of the B4328 and B4314. At one time this was also on the route of the mail coaches which travelled from London to Ireland via

Milford Haven. The local community here takes great pride in the village; in recent years Tavernspite has won awards in competitions for Wales In Bloom and Best Kept Village. Tavernspite is also notable for its chapel, one of the most remote and picturesque in Pembrokeshire.

LUDCHURCH

Located less than 3 miles south-east of Narberth, Ludchurch stands on the route of the Knightway footpath. A curious fact is that prior to the 1950's the name Ludchurch referred only to the Norman church and parish and the village itself was known as Egypt. There are definitely no pyramids here, but there are some fine lime kilns to be seen in the old quarry. The name Ludchurch is also becoming increasingly known among people with good taste. The reason is Princes Gate Water - a spring water of exceptionally pure quality which has proved so popular that it is now supplied all over Wales and to markets as far apart as London and North America. The water comes from 3 acres of farmland in the parish which are saturated with clear natural springs.

Tavernspite

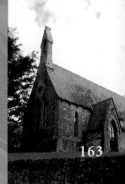

Templeton

163

CANASTON BRIDGE

Just west of Narberth Canaston Bridge marks the junctions of the A40 and A4075. This attractive wooded area is the northern boundary of the Eastern Cleddau and from here you can join the Knightsway - a 9 mile walk linking the Daugleddau Trail with the coast path at Amroth. Nearby, on the south side of the A40 is a picnic area and restored Blackpool Mill. A mile or so from the north side is the impressive ruins of Llawhaden Castle. A few miles south on the A4075 are the neighbouring attractions of Oakwood and CC2000. Also within the area are several interesting woodland walks, including a relatively short path which takes you to Blackpool Mill.

OAKWOOD & CC2000

One of the top ten theme parks in the UK, Oakwood has over 40 rides and attractions for all the family. Next door is CC2000, Oakwood's indoor bowling and family entertainment centre.

BLACKPOOL MILL

In a beautiful setting on the banks of the Eastern Cleddau, this is one of the finest examples in Wales of a mill complete with all of its machinery. You can visit their museum, gift shop and tea room.

for more information
tel: 01437 541233

Oakwood
Blackpool Mill

Oakwood

TEMPLETON

The layout of Templeton which is a mile south of Narberth, is a fine example of village planning in the Middle Ages. It is believed that the Knights Templars had a hospice here, possibly on the site now occupied by St. John's church, and in the 13th century the village was known as the settlement of the Templars. Hence the name Templeton today. There are several ancient sites here, including Sentence Castle, originally a raised fortification which also probably dates from the time of the Knights Templars. The Knightsway Trail passes through the village.

WISTON

The village of Wiston, five miles northeast of Haverfordwest, was an important settlement in medieval times. Wiston Castle was at a strategic point on the Landsker Line and as such was the scene of much bloodshed in the 12th and 13th centuries. The remains of this impressive motte and bailey castle are a short walk from the car park in the centre of the village and now administered by CADW. Admission is free.

THE DAUGLEDDAU

The Daugleddau estuary is an area of great natural beauty, comprising the fascinating stretch of waterway which extends inland from the Haven and encompasses four rivers Western Cleddau, Eastern Cleddau, Carew and Cresswell. It is an inner sanctuary, often described as the hidden treasure of the Pembrokeshire Coast National Park. Daugleddau (which means two

Beside the Daugleddau

165

The Daugleddau

Lawrenny

rivers at the Cleddau) begins east of the Cleddau tool bridge, and has become known as The Secret Waterway. In recognition of the Daugleddau's remarkable diversity of flora and fauna, many parts of the waterway are designated Sites of Special Scientific Interest. These include the Carew and Cresswell rivers, Lawrenny Wood, Minwear Wood, parts of Slebech Park and West Williamston Quarries. In Tudor times Lawrenny was famous for its oysters. By the 19th century sailing vessels of all shapes and sizes, brigantines, ketches, sloops, schooners and coasters, were busily importing and exporting coal, grain, limestone, timber and general goods. Towards the latter part of the century, Willy Boys (flat barge like craft) - carried local produce and ran a shuttle service between seagoing vessels and the Daugleddau's upper reaches. The poor acidic soils of West Wales made lime a valuable and highly saleable commodity. Limestone was quarried at West Williamston, Garron Pill and Llangwm Ferry and burned in hundreds of kilns along the waterway and coastline, from South Pembrokeshire to Cardigan Bay. The remains of several kilns are still visible. The band of carboniferous coal measures which runs across Pembrokeshire from St. Bride's Bay to Saundersfoot cuts through the uppermost reaches of the Daugleddau, and mining around Landshipping was at its height in the first half of the 19th century, particularly after the introduction in 1800 of the first steam engine to be used in a Pembrokeshire coalfield. The high quality anthracite was in great demand. A tragic accident at the Garden Pit near Landshipping in 1844 and a series of insurmountable geological problems which plagued the coalfield throughout its working life led to a rapid decline of the industry by the early 20th century. The last colliery to work, at Hook on the Western Cleddau, was closed by the National Coal Board in 1949. The waterway's rich oak woodlands helped encourage boatbuilding and cutters, smacks and schooners were built at yards and quays along the Daugleddau. At Lawrenny alone, over 40 sailing vessels were built during the first half of the 19th century.

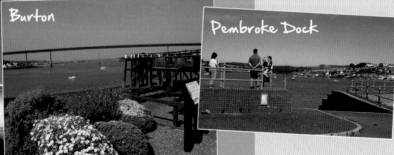

Burton

Pembroke Dock

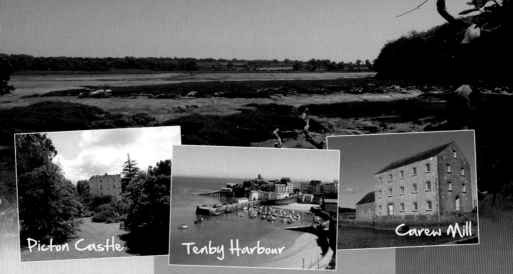

Picton Castle

Tenby Harbour

Carew Mill

Other industries flourished too, from a chemical works at Whalecomb to a furnace and forge which operated on the site now occupied by Blackpool Mill. During the 19th century over 100 men earned their living by compass net fishing, a traditional method, suited to rivers with fast flowing tidal currents, which required considerable skill and courage. Much of the working life of the Daugleddau centred around Lawrenny Quay, which in its heyday had more than one quay. Today it is noted for its Yacht Station and excellent facilities for pleasure craft and seeing the waterway from the comfort of a boat will take you to places inaccessible by any other means. Whatever your method of exploration, the Daugleddau will provide endless relaxation and enjoyment. Sights worth seeking out are many and varied, including Lawrenny village and its well restored cottages and huge Norman church. A National Park picnic site gives superb views over the Carew and Cresswell rivers. At Cresswell Quay, a picnic site and pub are just yards from the water's edge where Kingfishers and herons feed in full view. The long distance Daugleddau Trail and other footpaths reveal a succession of delights, from the evocative ruins of magnificent Carew Castle to the ancient woodland of Minwear. There are many other historic sites to enjoy, such as the exotic gardens of Upton Castle and Picton Castle and the restored mills at Carew and Blackpool. The lime stone quarries have long since fallen silent, but today West Williamston is the centre of other important work for the waterway, the rescue, nursing and rehabilitation of injured and contaminated seabirds, at the Oiled Bird Rescue Centre. Regular visitors to the centre each year are substantial numbers of Manx shearwaters, which once blown inland by autumn gales are unable to take off again and are often stranded in brightly lit harbours and resorts such as Tenby.

Quayside Lawrenny Tearoom

167

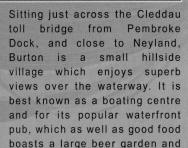

BURTON

Sitting just across the Cleddau toll bridge from Pembroke Dock, and close to Neyland, Burton is a small hillside village which enjoys superb views over the waterway. It is best known as a boating centre and for its popular waterfront pub, which as well as good food boasts a large beer garden and panoramic views over the estuary to the south, east and west.

Burton

CAREW

The most southerly point of the Daugleddau section of the National Park, Carew is famous for its magnificent riverside castle, fine Celtic cross and restored tidal mill. There is also a picnic site and car park here, accessible from the village across the old narrow bridge. The village itself is small, neat and has a distinct charm, with a pub and a bridge. The village itself is small, neat and has a distinct charm, with a pub and arestaurant offering plenty of local hospitality. Close to Carew, on the south side of the A477, is the slumbering hamlet of Carew Cheriton. The church here dates from the late 14th century and is distinctive for its very tall tower, which has a corner steeple. In the church-yard there is a detached mortuary chapel.

Carew
Castle

CAREW CASTLE

Here is a castle which has everything: magnificent ruins, an evocative setting, a long and important history, examples of medieval and Elizabethan architecture, a Celtic cross which is one of the finest in Wales and archaeological deposits dating back over the last 2000 years Carew is undoubtedly a king among castles. It stands on a low limestone ridge at the head of a tidal inlet of the Carew river - a strategic position, as it guarded a crossing of the river and the main road to Pembroke, 5 miles away. In times of war it could also be supplied by boat, as it has access to the open sea via the Daugleddau and the Haven waterway. Carew Castle was occupied continuously from the 12th century to the end of the 17th century, during which time it was gradually transformed from a medieval fortress to an Elizabethan mansion of consid erable splendour. Most photo-graphs today tend to emphasise the latter, as the castle is often shot from across the water of Carew Pill to capture on of the ruin's most striking features - the great Renaissance north wing. which Sir John Perrot began building in 1588. Perrot died in 1592 of natural causes while imprisoned in the Tower of London and the wing was never completed. In April 1507 the castle and nearby Carew Meadows were the site of the Great Tournament - a spectacu-lar 5 day event, attended by over 600 noblemen. The occasion was in honour of the Tudor monarchy and also to celebrate the fact that Henry VII had bestowed upon Sir Rhys ap Thomas, who held the castle at the time, the Order of the Knight of the Garter. Sir Rhys had played a major part in Henry's victory at Bosworth and was knighted on the battlefield; it is even said that Richard III died at his hands. Although the king himself was not in attendance, the tournament was a grand affair on a scale not previously seen in Wales. The huge assembly enjoyed jousting, sword displays, hunting and other sports of the day, and the Great Hall was the scene of a sumptuous banquet. This was the last event of its kind ever staged in Britain. During the Civil War years of 1644 and 1645, the castle changed hands between royalist and parliamentarian forces no fewer than four times. Towards the end of the century it was abandoned by the Carew family and fell into decline. The exciting thing about Carew Castle is that much is still being discovered about its very early history. Since 1986 it has been the subject of a phased but very intensive archaeological survey involving excavation, a stone by stone study of the surviving walls and buildings and examination of documents. To date, two major surprises have been unearthed. One is that the Norman part of the castle is much bigger and older than previously suspected. The other discovery of pre-Norman fortifications, adding weight to speculation that the site had a royal significance long before the Normans arrived and was the seat of Welsh

kings throughout the Roman and Dark Age periods. This idea is supported by the famous Carew Cross, which stands within the Castle Field and is a memorial to a Welsh king who died in 1035, more than half a century before the Normans took Pembroke in 1093. In the near future, visitors to the castle will be able to see some of the discoveries made by the archaeological survey, as there are plans to build an Interpretation Centre on site. The castle is still privately owned by descendants of the Carew family, but is leased to the Pembrokeshire Coast National Park Authority under a 99 year agreement so that the castle and its surrounding earthworks can be conserved for everyone's enjoyment. Carew is the only castle managed by the National Park Authority.

for more
information
tel: 01646 651782

CAREW CROSS

Carew's famous 11th century Celtic Cross stands close to the castle. It is a royal memorial commemorating Maredudd ap Edwin, who in 1033 became joint ruler with his brother of Deheubarth, the kingdom of southwest Wales. Just two years later he was killed in battle. The cross comprises two separate pieces and the inscriptions are predominantly Celtic but also reflect Scandinavian influence.

Carew
Castle

Carew
Cross

169

Open daily April to October 10.00am to 5.00pm

CAREW
CASTLE & TIDAL MILL

Situated on the banks of the Carew River, the magnificent Norman castl
and only restored tidal mill in Wales are linked by a round walk.
Close by is Carew Cross, one of the finest in Wales
(CADW guardianship).
Signposted off the A477 Kilgetty to Pembroke Dock.
Tel: Carew Castle (01646) 651782
enquiries@carewcastle.com   www.carewcastle.com
Check out our website for winter opening times and events listing

Daily guided tours • family activities & ever
gift shops • picnic areas • walks

Site managed by Pembrokeshire Coast National Park Authority

CAREW TIDAL MILL

This is the only tidal mill to remain intact in Wales, and it stands on the causeway which dams the 23 acre millpond. The present mill is 19th century but the site was previously occupied by a medieval building which operated in Elizabethan times. The mill's machinery was powered by water stored at flood tide and released through sluices to drive two undershot mill wheels. It continued to grind commercially until 1937 and was restored in 1972. Today it is often known as the French mill - a reference to either the architectural style of the building or the mill's grinding stones imported from France. As with Carew Castle the mill is managed by the National Park Authority. It is open to visitors throughout the season and is a popular and fascinating attraction.

for more information
tel: 01646 651782

UPTON CASTLE GROUNDS
Cosheston Nr Pembroke

Upton Castle grounds and gardens occupy a secluded wooded valley which runs down to a tributary of the Carew River. The grounds contain over 250 different species of trees and shrubs.

CRESSWELL QUAY

This is a beautiful spot for a picnic, or to enjoy a pint or Sunday lunch at the old riverside pub. The tidal Cresswell River attracts herons and a variety of other waders and brilliantly coloured kingfishers often catch the eye as they dive for prey and seek out the best perches along the banks. Across the water, high above the steep wooded slopes, buzzards soar effortlessly over the trees of Scotland Wood.

HOOK

There is much evidence here of the area's long and intensive coalmining activities, including the remains of two quays, tramways and bellshaped mines from the 17th and 18th centuries. Hook pit did not close until 1949 and in its later days was linked to the Milford Haven railway. It is a small settlement on the eastern banks of the Daugleddau, near the confluence of the Western

Carew
Tidal
Mill

Upton
Castle
Gardens

171

INLAND PEMBROKESHIRE

and Eastern Cleddau rivers. Across the river, close to Picton Point is the site from which the Picton Ferry once operated. Coal was a valuable commodity here as the mining industry thrived for a period in the 19th century and Landshipping Quay exported coal from several pits. Close by is the site of the terrible Garden Pit colliery disaster of 1844, when high tide flooded the mine and 40 lives were lost, including those of several young boys.

an 18th century mansion now demolished - the National Park Authority did establish a picnic area. Please note however that this area has been in private ownership since 1995 and is no longer open to the public. Earlier last century, at Lawrenny House Farm, Mr. J.F. Lort-Phillips trained racehorses and put the village on the map when Kirkland won the Grand National in 1905. Another horseracing connection, nearby Coedcanlas was the birthplace of famous jockey turned best selling author Dick Francis.

LAWRENNY

Lawrenny has an impressive church with a large Norman tower. Using the Site once occupied by Lawrenny Castle -

LAWRENNY QUAY

Close to Lawrenny village, Lawrenny Quay is a popular area for boating which once

Quayside Tearooms

boasted a thriving shipbuilding industry. During the Second World War, Lawrenny Quay served as a marine air base for 764 Squadron of the Fleet Air Arm. Up to 15 Walrus seaplanes could be seen moored on the river, and the officers were billeted at Lawrenny Castle.

LLANGWM

Llangwm has a long history, and is said to have been a Flemish settlement in the Middle Ages. Traditionally the main occupations of the villagers were oyster and herring fishing, with mining rising in importance in the 19th century. Llangwm is well known for its reputedly tough breed of fisherwomen, who until this century were a familiar sight on Pembrokeshire roads, carrying baskets of fish on their heads to sell in the towns. Near to Llangwm is Black Tar, a popular spot for boating and watersport enthusiasts.

MARTLETWY

A small agricultural community east of Landshipping, Martletwy is now the unlikely home of a vineyard - Cwm Deri

- the only commercial vineyard in Pembrokeshire. Another product associated with Martletwy is coal, though this industry has long since vanished. Among the interesting historic buildings here is the church.

MINWEAR

A large area of the precious and ancient Minwear Wood is a designated SSSI - Site of Special Scientific Interest and in the heart of the wood is the 12th century church. Close by are the ruins of the medieval Sisters' Houses, which once accommodated pilgrims bound for the monastic community at St. Davids. Minwear Wood is close to Blackpool Mill and Canaston Bridge.

WEST WILLIAMSTON

When the limestone quarries were established here, this medieval farming hamlet was transformed into a busy quarrymen's village with smithies, inns and its own church. Today the area has reverted to farming, and is also the home of the important Oiled Bird Rescue Centre.

Lawrenny

Llangwm

Cwm Deri Vineyard

173

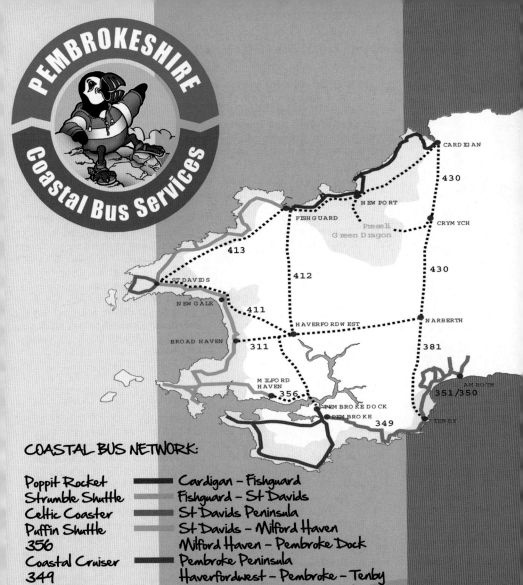

PEMBROKESHIRE Coastal Bus Services

COASTAL BUS NETWORK:

Poppit Rocket		Cardigan – Fishguard
Strumble Shuttle		Fishguard – St Davids
Celtic Coaster		St Davids Peninsula
Puffin Shuttle		St Davids – Milford Haven
356		Milford Haven – Pembroke Dock
Coastal Cruiser		Pembroke Peninsula
349		Haverfordwest – Pembroke – Tenby
350/351		Tenby – Saundersfoot – Amroth

FEEDER ROUTES:

412		Cardigan – Haverfordwest
Preseli Green Dragon		Crymych – Newport
411/413		Fishguard – Haverfordwest
311		Haverfordwest – Broad Haven
315		Haverfordwest – Milford Haven – Dale
381		Haverfordwest – Narberth – Tenby
430		Tenby – Narberth – Cardigan

INLAND PEMBROKESHIRE

PUFFIN SHUTTLE

St. Davids - Milford Haven.
The route passes through the beautiful sights of Newgale, Broad Haven, Little Haven, Marloes and Dale, so all you have to do is sit back and enjoy the ride

CELTIC COASTER

Around the St. Davids Peninsula.
This 14 seater minibus runs from St. Davids to Porthclais, St. Justinians and Whitesands, enabling you to walk the Peninsula, catch the boat trips to Ramsey island or enjoy a day on the beach. The bus can carry 1 x wheelchair.

STRUMBLE SHUTTLE

St Davids - Fishguard
The bus takes you to Abereiddy beach, Porthgain, Trefin, Mathry, Tregwnt Woolen Mill (for Porth Mawr beach) St Nicholas, Trefasser Cross (for Pwll Deri YHA) and as close to Stumble Head as we can get before taking you into Goodwick and Fishguard.

POPPIT ROCKET

Fishguard - Cardigan
Calling at Pwllgwaelod, Newport, Moylegrove, Poppit Sands (for the start of the coast path) and St Dogmaels.

Service subject to change please click on
www.pembrokeshire.gov.uk/transport
for details and information or pick up leaflet from any TIC

COASTAL CRUISER

This bus runs out of Pembroke to Angle, Bosherston, Stackpole and Freshwater East. Look out for the new colourful buses that display the 'Puffin Logo' and the eye-catching Puffin bus stops. This means that they are part of the coastal bus network. Catching a bus in Pembrokeshire is easy. You don't even have to find the bus stops as all as all the Coastal Buses are on a 'Hail an Ride' so all you have to do is signal to the driver to stop. Passengers can be picked up and set down at any point along the bus route providing it is safe to do so. Once on board your driver will have plenty of local knowledge to help you find your destination or recommend one.

TRY BEFORE YOU BUY - COASTAL BUSES NOW ON FILM

Have you ever thought about catching the Coastal Bus to access a beach, to start your walk or even just to enjoy the scenery, but weren't sure if it's for you? Well, why not try before you buy. Now you can view Pembrokeshire's beautifully scenery from the comfort of your armchair. The views are amazing and it will inspire you to go. Visit www.pembrokeshire.gov.uk/transport click on Coastal Buses and choose your journey. If you do not have access to a computer call in to one of Pembrokeshire's Tourist Information Centres or drop a line to:

Pembrokeshire Greenways
Transport & Environment
County Hall
Haverfordwest
SA61 1TP

and we will send you a DVD.

Did you know?

Coastal buses run on recycled vegetable oil

The Coastal Cruiser, Puffin Shuttle, Celtic Coaster, Pocket Rocket and Strumble Shuttle coastal bus services run 7 days a week during the holiday season with a reduced service in the winter. In the south of the county local bus services provide a year round service.

PRESELI HILLS WALKER'S BUS

If you are heading to the Preseli Hills this summer then look out for the improved walkers' bus service. The Gwaun Valley bus serving Fishguard, Cligwyn, to Bwlch y Groes and the second Preselli Hills service will travel between Crymych Mynachlogddu, Rosebush to Bwylch y Groes. These services have ongoing connections and are an important link for walkers and tourists connecting the mountains with the coast.

Details are available from:
www.prta.co.uk

TAKE THE TRAIN FOR A WALK

This summer why not use the train to get yourself around Pembrokeshire. The Greenways "Walk and Ride" leaflets detail walks from Whitland, Narberth, Saundersfoot, Tenby, Manorbier, Lamphey, Haverfordwest and Milford Haven train stations. It also includes walks by bus in the Preseli Hills and St. Dogmaels. Pembrokeshire Greenways is a project that encourages people to access the countryside through walking, cycling, bus and train travel.

for details and information pick up a leaflet from any TIC, or tel: 01437 764551

PEMBROKESHIRE'S ISLANDS & WILDLIFE

Pembrokeshire certainly has many virtues, one of its main attractions is the outstanding natural beauty of its coastline and surrounding islands. The wildlife to be found in the area is a major reason for the large number of visitors. The islands such as Ramsey, Grassholm and Skomer are positively teeming with extraordinary wildlife, on land, in the sea and in the air.

RAMSEY ISLAND

260 hectares of fascinating island, now accessible by a regular boat service from the lifeboat slip at St. Justinian's, about three miles west of St. Davids. The island is across the infamous but spectacular Ramsey Sound, with its equally infamous and treacherous reef known as The Bitches. Ramsey was farmed until very recently. To the east, steep sheltered spring fed valleys and cliffs are covered in a wonderful tangle of rich vegetation. To the north east are sheep grazed fields. Ramsey is the only Pembrokeshire island with breeding lapwings. Chough also find Ramsey extremely attractive and both species breed and winter here in good numbers. The western coastline is rugged and spectacular with two small mountains, Carn Llundain and Carn Ysgubor, sheltering the island from the main blast of the prevailing westerly winds. The island is also home to several thousand seabirds in the season, including razorbills, kittiwakes, fulmars and guillemots. On a clear day the mountain top views are superb. To the north and east are St. Davids and the Preseli Hills. To the west, the rocks and islets of the Bishops and Clerks and the main South Bishop rock, where Manx shearwaters and storm petrels breed. To the south, the small offshore islands of Ynys Cantwr and Ynys Beri with Skomer and Midland Isle beyond them across St. Bride's Bay. The caves and beaches around Ramsey are breeding grounds for the largest population of grey seals in southwestern Britain. More than 300 seal pups are born here each season. In 1992 the Royal Society for the Protection of Birds bought Ramsey. There is now a resident warden on the island, who meets every visitor, though there are necessary restrictions on the number of people allowed on the island each day. For those lucky enough to make it, there is a reception centre, refreshments toilets and a shop. Unpaid assistant wardens can arrange to stay and help with work on the reserve.

lifeboat slip at St. Justinian's

VOYAGES OF DISCOVERY

The Ramsey Island Boat Booking Office, opposite Lloyds TSB Bank in the centre of St. Davids

tel: 0800 854367
or
01437 721911

If you mention Dolphins to most people they immediately think of the captive animals that perform tricks in Sea-life Parks. Tell them that you are going Whale and Dolphin watching and they assume you have to jet off to some exotic location in a far-flung corner of the globe.

Well they would be wrong; Pembrokeshire's coastal waters are home to large numbers of these enigmatic creatures and sightings of several hundred animals at a time have been recorded.

The nutrient - rich waters flowing in from the Atlantic produce a prolific ecosystem noted as a Site of Special Scientific Interest. Here on the edge of the Celtic Deep is one of the few places in the UK where cetaceans, seals and birdlife can be found in large numbers. As well as hundreds of Common Dolphin, sightings include Minkie, Sei and Fin Whale. Bottlenose Dolphin, Orca, Rissos Dolphin, and the occasional Basking Shark.

During the winter months some of these animals can be seen off many of our headlands, where the strong tidal currents pull up nutrients from the sea bed providing food for the shoals of fish on which they feed.

For close encounters a boat trip out to deeper waters can produce some breathtaking scenes. Dolphins are a highly intelligent and very social animal and will very often seek out contact with vessels.

Typically, calves are born in early summer. A single calf is produced every 3 years or so after a gestation period of around a year. The calf suckles for 2 or more years, but starts to eat fish within 3 months and during summer months mothers with young calves have been observed in 'nursery groups' swimming along with vessels for short periods, as if introducing their calves to the correct etiquette for contact with humans. These calves will stay with their mothers for up to 5 years, learning the complex social skills needed to be part of Dolphin society.

To try to describe the emotions experienced when observing these magnificent creatures in their wild and natural state would exhaust a dictionary. The exhilaration as Dolphin bow ride, play and generally show off to their audience, leaping completely out of the water as they race along side you almost close enough to touch will leave you breathless.

Voyages **of Discovery**

Wildlife Voyages to the North Pembrokeshire Islands and Offshore Whale and Dolphin Expeditions

Ramsey Island Voyage A one to one and a half hour tour around the RSPB reserve. Spectacular sea caves, large colonies of grey seals, porpoises and bird colonies. Fully guided a FAMILY FAVOURITE.

North Bishops Puffin and Shearwater Voyage
An evening 1½ hour voyage to the Bishops and Clerks Puffin Isles. Excellent seal watching and thousands of migratory shearwaters and not forgetting the puffins.

Offshore Islands Whale and Dolphin Watch
First offshore to Grassholm Island, home to the second largest gannet colony in the N. Hemisphere, then a sweep of these distant waters looking for cetaceans. Last year provided excellent sightings of dolphin (over 500 seen on one voyage), porpoise, Minke whale, Orca and Fin whale.

Family, group and educational discounts - Suitable for all ages

Booking at our own friendly and dedicated office
THE RAMSEY ISLAND BOAT BOOKING OFFICE
Opposite Lloyds Bank in the centre of St. Davids
FREEPHONE **0800 854 367**
Tel. **01437 721 911** *www.ramseyisland.co.uk*

Voyages Of Discovery have pioneered Cetacean watching off the Pembrokeshire coast for several years. A family run company with a fleet of specially built RHIB's crewed by expert conservationists, fully guided wildlife tours are run all year round. Offshore Island Voyages to the Grassholm Gannet colony and including Whale and Dolphin watching, run from the end of May to late September.

For more information call their booking office or visit the website:
www.ramseyisland.co.uk

181

CARDIGAN ISLAND

A small island of less than 16 hectares, situated at the mouth of the River Teifi. The island is leased by The Wildlife Trust of South and West Wales, who annually census its small colonies of seabirds. The lesser black-backed gulls are the dominant species, with only a few hundred herring gulls and very small numbers of other seabirds. In 1934, when the motor vessel Herefordshire was wrecked on the northern rocks, brown rats came ashore and annihilated the islands population of puffins. There have been various attempts to reinstate both puffins and Manx shearwaters. A few have been bred but it is a long and slow process to establish healthy breeding colonies here again.

GRASSHOLM

Situated around eleven miles offshore, Grassholm is a reserve of the Royal Society for the Protection of Birds, and is the only Gannet colony in Wales. Viewed from afar the island appears to be snow covered or having a white halo, this in fact is the Gannet colony. Approximately 34,000 pairs of Gannets crowd into the tiny, waterless island to lay their single egg. The noise and sheer spectacle of vast numbers of these magnificent seabirds is something that once experienced can never be forgotten. Gannets are brilliant white in colour and dive for fish in the waters around Grassholm from heights of up to 30 metres. When one realises that a full grown Gannet is about the size of the average Christmas goose the spectacle becomes even more amazing. Writer Dr. Brian John describes the scene thus; "there can be few more beautiful sights than Gannets diving close inshore, wheeling and swooping on the bright clean wind of a Pembrokeshire summer day". The second largest Gannet colony in Britain, Grassholm is a major success story. In 1924 there were 1,000 pairs recorded on the island to an officially recorded 32,000 pairs in 2005. Although Gannets dominate the island to such a degree that even from the mainland it has been described as resembling an iced bun. Other breeding birds include small numbers of Kittiwake,

Razorbill and Shag together with Herring and Great Black-backed Gulls. From the boats that take visitors around the island there are often sightings of porpoise, basking shark and even the occasional sunfish. Plus of course a variety of birds such as Puffin or Shearwater, which may be resident on the other neighbouring islands.

SKOMER ISLAND

This is the largest of Pembrokeshire's islands, a National Nature Reserve owned by the Countryside Council for Wales but run by The Wildlife Trust of South and West Wales, who employ a permanent warden and staff. The island ferry runs from Martin's Haven on the Marloes Peninsula every day except Monday, though during bank holidays the island is open to visitors all the time. There is a charge for the boat trip and also for landing, but children under 16 are exempt from the latter. There are guided tours around Skomer, usually operated by the National Park Authority, but in the main visitors are greeted and given a brief informative talk, which includes information on where to find all of the island's interesting sights and wildlife. From then until the boats leave in the afternoon, you are free to explore via the well defined footpaths. Skomer has some very well preserved archaeological remains dating back to the early Iron Age, in the form of standing stones, hut circles, burial cairns, walls and numerous lynchets. The island was farmed until the mid 1950's, but is now grazed only by rabbits, albeit thousands of them. The flora is not rich, but the carpets of spring and early summer flowering bluebells, red campion, white sea campion and thrift are some of the most colourful in the west. The island's cliff scenery is spectacular, both scenically and for its many thousands of breeding guillemots, Razorbills, Kittiwakes and Fulmars. More than 10,000 pairs of lesser Black-backed Gulls nest in the middle of the island, the largest colony of this species in Europe. Other gulls, such as the Greater Black-backed and Herring are also well represented. Skomer, in fact, boasts the largest colony of breeding seabirds in southern Britain. This is in spite of many years farming activity during which no species of ground predators, even rats or cats, ever managed to establish themselves. Hence ground and burrow nesting sites are numerous. There are over 10,000 puffins and at least 100,000 Manx shearwaters, the world's biggest colony. Of the ground nesting birds, there are good numbers of short-eared owls, curlews and oystercatchers, to name but a few.

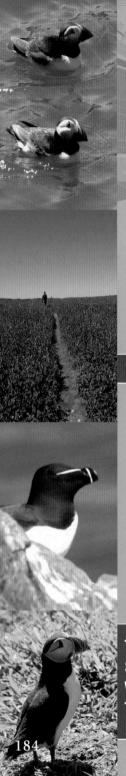

The island is also home to a unique island race of bank voles, common shrews and wood mice, and on the beaches during the autumn over 150 grey seal pups are born, making this the second most important seal breeding colony in southwestern Britain. Another notable colony is that established by shags on Midland Island, a much smaller island south of Skomer. Skomer, Grassholm and Skokholm are all included in a Special Protection Area designated by a European directive, a further indication of the value of Pembrokeshre's offshore islands to international wildlife.

SKOKHOLM

This small island has been owned by the Dale Castle Estates since the 1970's and is now leased by The Wildlife Trust of South and West Wales, who employ a cook and a warden. There is full board accommodation for up to 16 people a week. Skokholm has all the richness and profusion of wildlife and beauty of Skomer, but in a smaller more gentle

way. The only seabird not common to both is the Kittiwake, and in the quarry on the westerly cliffs below the lighthouse there is a colony of several thousand storm petrels, the largest colony in the Irish Sea. In 1936 the island was set up as Britain's first ever bird observatory by a group of people which included Ronald (R.M) Lockley. This of course is Lockley's Dream Island, which was occupied and farmed by him until 1940.

ST. MAGARET'S ISLAND

St. Margaret's Island and its much bigger neighbour Caldey, lay some way to the south of the county. The island has the largest colony of cormorants in Wales, located on top of its steep limestone cliffs, while other seabirds include Greater Black-backed and Herring Gulls, Guillemots, Razorbills, Kittiwakes and Fulmars on the vertical cliffs. There are very few puffins, but burrow nesting birds are restricted by the presence of rats. The island

There are limited sailings to Skokholm Island, for details contact: Wildlife Trust of South West Wales Tel: 01239 621600

Caldey Monastery

Caldey Lighthouse

and its wildlife and the coastline of Caldey are best seen from one of the pleasure boat, which run regularly from Tenby harbour between April and early Autumn, but no landings are allowed on St. Magaret's.

CALDEY ISLAND

Caldey is owned and run by the small community of Cistercian monks, who farm the island with the help of a few people in the village. A day out here is totally different from anything else you will experience in Pembrokeshire. Several boats a day take many curious visitors to this atmospheric and religious centre, and landings and access are simple compared to other islands. Leaving the boat you will walk towards the village and monastery passing Priory Beach, a beautiful, gently curving stretch of sand backed by dunes, and the island's only safe bathing beach. The easy stroll up through the trees has a distinctly Mediterranean feel to it, which is emphasied when you see the monastery. The imposing but attractive monastic buildings are all whitewashed and have terracotta roofs. The village itself has everything to offer visitors including shops and a cafe with open air seating under swaying whispering trees.

Visit a world *of* island wildlife

Grassholm · Skomer · Skokholm

Pembrokeshire Islands

Operated by **Dale Sailir**

The Of Skon Landing
nat WILDLIFE

Wildlife voyages by RIB

Dale Sea Safaris – to **Grassholm** or **Skomer** and **Skokholm** – an exhilarating sea adventure on a fast, safe rigid hulled inflatable boat that will allow you to **experience the incredible, breathtaking sights of the sea birds, seals and dolphins** – sights and memories that will live with you forever.

$2^{1}/_{2}$**hr trips: Skomer and Skokholm 9.30, 3.30 & 6.30, Grassholm 12.30**
Adults £30.00 Children (under 14) £15.00 – booking required

Info and booking: **01646 603123** OR 01646 603110 / 01646 603109

Land on **Skomer Island**

Dale Princess Skomer Landing Trips – a 15 minute boat ride takes you on to the island of Skomer – a world dedicated to wildlife including the famous puffins, grey seals, guillemots, razorbills, fulmars, cormorants, shags and shearwaters. Depart Martin's Haven SA62 3BJ. Closed 17, 18 & 19 May

Landing Trips depart 10.00, 11.00, 12.00 excl Mon (runs Bank Hols) no booking required
Boat fee £10.00 (child £7.00), landing fee £8.00 (child FREE, senior citizen £7.00, student £4.00)

Round Skomer Cruises – depart Tues, Wed, Thurs, Fri, Sat, Sun at 1.00pm.
Depart Mon at 10.30, 11.45. Bank Hol Mon at 1.00pm only. £10.00 (child £7.00) no booking required

Info: **01646 603123** OR 01646 603110 / 01646 603109

We also run Wildlife Cruises around Grassholm Island and landing trips to Skokholm Island aboard the larger 'Dale Princess' – booking required.

AS SEEN ON TV's Coast, the One Show and Countryfile

www.pembrokeshireislands.co.uk E-mail: enquiries@pembrokeshireislands.co.uk

PEMBROKESHIRE ARTS & CRAFTS

Pembrokeshire is well known for its wealth of creative talent with an array of arts and crafts as diverse as the landscape. So whether it's candle making, wood turning, paintings, photography or pottery you're after you will find it all here in fabulous Pembrokeshire. The following is a brief guide to just some of the many attractions to be found across the county.

MAP PG 3

TENBY MUSEUM & ART GALLERY

CASTLE HILL, TENBY, SA70 7BP, Tel: 01834 842809
www.tenbymuseum.org.uk

Established in 1878, this award winning
museum has two art galleries with
regular changing exhibitions.
Open throughout the year.

TENBY MUSEUM & ART GALLERY

AMGUEDDFA AC ORIEL
GELF DINBYCH-Y-PYSGOD

SEE ADVERT PAGE 21

 MAP PG 3

LION STREET ART GALLERY

1, WHITE LION STREET, TENBY, SA70 7ES, Tel: 01834 843375
www.artmatters.org.uk

Paintings and original prints together
with some sculpture and ceramics by
some of the best Welsh and British
artists in a uniquely relaxed and
welcoming environment.

 MAP PG 3

A GIFT OF GLASS

CNR. TRAFALGAR & UPPER PARK RD, TENBY, SA70 7DW
Tel: 07880 953544, Email: info@giftofglass.com

•Come and see the glassblower
•Gifts for all occasions
•Handcrafted ornamental glassware
•Open 7 days

 6 MAP PG 3

THE CORNSTORE

THE GREEN, PEMBROKE, SA71 4NU
Tel: 01646 684 290

Two floors of beautiful home furnishings,
funiture and accessories. Local crafts, art
displays and visit our jewellery room.

THE OLD SMITHY

SIMPSON CROSS, HAVERFORDWEST, SA62 6EP
Tel: 01437 710628

Welsh crafts and gifts including
Welsh Royal Crystal, Pembertons
Chocolates, Caldey Island products,and
Celtic Jewellery. We also have a
purpose built gallery showing local artists.

SEE ADVERT PAGE 72

HILTON COURT GARDENS & CRAFTS

ROCH, HAVERFORDWEST, SA62 6AE, Tel: 01437 710262
www.hiltongardensandcrafts.co.uk

The Crafts Centre is housed in a group of
restored stables. Here you will find among
the craft shops, a working pottery, photography,
gallery and framing facility offering fabulous
and unusual gifts, allowing you to shop in a
relaxed and creative atmosphere.

THE ANDREW BAILEY GALLERY

23 THE RIVERSIDE SHOPPING CENTRE, HAVERFORDWEST
SA61 2LJ, Tel: 01437 766889

Andrew's gallery in Haverfordwest's Riverside Shopping
Centre sells only his own original watercolours and prints.
He puts on seven exhibitions in the Pembrokeshire area
each year including a summer one-man show at St David's
Cathedral.

Andrew Bailey
International Award Winning Artist

Watercolour Paintings & Limited
Edition Prints from
Pembrokeshire, West Wales

WINDOW ON WALES - SOLVA & ST DAVIDS

MAIN ST, SOLVA, HAVERFORDWEST - Tel: 01437 720659
2 CROSS SQUARE, ST. DAVIDS, HAVERFORDWEST - Tel: 01437 721492

Window On Wales has two branches, in Solva
and St Davids, both being housed in traditional stone
buildings, which are filled with wide ranges
of clothes and gifts deliberately chosen to be
unlike the High Street.

SOLVA POTTERY

SOLVA POTTERY, MAIN STREET, SOLVA, SA62 6UU, Tel: 01437 720516

Situated in the centre of the harbour village of Lower Solva, Solva Pottery was established in 1984 by Colin and Bobbie Jacobs. Here we produce Pottery in beautiful turquoise shades, Batik and Hand Painted Clothes, Ties and Cushions, Cards and Lamp Shades, all made on the premises.

RAUL SPEEK GALLERY

THE OLD CHAPEL, MAIN STREET, SOLVA, SA62 6UU
Tel: 01437 721907, www.raulspeek.co.uk

I consider myself fortunate both to have been born into the Cuban revolution process and to be able to express myself as an artist. To date some of my best work has been acquired by different public and private collections around the world.In the present I live and work in a beautiful location in Solva, Pembrokeshire where you can come to experience my work.

ST DAVIDS STUDIO GALLERY

14 NUN STREET, ST DAVIDS, SA62 6NS, Tel: 01437 720648
www.stdavidsstudiogallery.co.uk

Located in Great Britain's smallest city, St Davids Studio Gallery occupies the ground floor and walled garden of a Georgian house just off St Davids' city square. We have the work of around 50 artists and makers on permanent display, some of whom you will recognise as established names and others who are less well known.

St Davids
Studio Gallery

ORIEL Y PARC

ST DAVIDS, SA62 6NW, Tel: 01437 720392, www.orielyparc.co.uk

We stock an interesting selection of locally produced items, including handmade jewellery, wooden bowls, lovespoons and cards. We also have an excellent selection of art books and supplies including paints, brushes and pastels. We have ordnance survey maps and walking guides, souvenirs, postcards and a wide selection of books including local history, Welsh interest and children's books. We also have educational toys for children.

ORIEL-Y-FELIN GALLERY

MAP PG 3 11

5 NUN ST, ST. DAVIDS, SA62 6NS, Tel: 01437 720386,
www.oriel-y-felin.com

This exciting gallery, new to St. Davids, showing wonderful work from local and invited artists. Pembrokeshire's only gallery showing original work by Pauline Beynon and Susie Grindey. There really is something for everyone - from the serious collector to those wanting unique, tempting, affordable art.

JANES OF FISHGUARD YARNS & CRAFTS

MAP PG 3 14

14-18 HIGH STREET, SA65 9AR,
Tel: 01348 874443,
www.janes-fishguard.co.uk

We offer a large selection of yarns a must visit for those keen knitters. Also beads, jewellery making accessories, Dylon, buttons galore and much more!

Yarns ~ Crafts
Haberdashery

Janes of Fishguard

For the widest selection of
Yarns & Crafts for miles!!

THE STUDIO AT PENRALLT

MAP PG 3 15

PENRALLT FARM, NEWPORT, SA42 0QE, Tel: 01239 820791
www.thestudioatpenrallt.co.uk

The Studio at Penrallt is owned by Helen Beazley, artist and author (the writer of the Lavender Road series - written as Helen Carey) and her husband, Marc Mordey. Helen's art is based on her interest in wildlife, architectural detail - particularly old buildings, and an abstract vision of the beautiful places in Wales and beyond. Marc specialises in quirky photographs and photocards which he sells under the Reasons to be Cheerful label.

PENRALLT GARDEN CENTRE & NURSERY

MAP PG 3 43

MOYLEGROVE, CARDIGAN, SA43 3BX
Tel: 01239 881295
www.penralltnursery.co.uk

Selling framed photographs, cards, paintings and also a wide range of wall art.

PEMBROKESHIRE CASTLES & MUSEUMS

Pembrokeshire is not only rich in beautiful scenery, it also has more than its fair share of historic castles and ancient sites together with museums to suit visitors of all ages.

Carew Castle

CAREW CASTLE

Carew is one of Pembrokeshire's finest castles with a wealth of detail and atmosphere. Owned and administered by the Pembrokeshire National Park Authority, to get there take the A477 from Pembroke Dock; or the Haverfordwest to St. Clears road, then turn off the A4075.

tel: 01646 651782
see advert page 170

LLAWHADEN CASTLE

Llawhaden is one of the Landsker castles along the Landsker Line, which is claimed to have divided North and South Pembrokeshire. It fell into disrepair in the mid 16th century after being used as a bishop's residence. Owned and administered by CADW, it can be reached via the A40 from Haverfordwest or St. Clears, then B4313

tel: 02920 500200

HAVERFORDWEST CASTLE

Haverfordwest Castle, which overlooks the town, was once used as a prison and more recently as a police station. Owned and administered by Pembrokeshire County Council. It now houses a small museum and the County Records Office.

tel: 01437 763087
see advert page 75

MANORBIER CASTLE

Manorbier Castle

Manorbier Castle is where the BBC filmed part of the children's series "The Lion the Witch and the Wardrobe". Set in a stunning area, it can be reached off the A4139 five miles from Tenby.

tel: 01834 871394
see advert page 33

193.

CILGERRAN CASTLE

Cilgerran Castle, three miles southeast of Cardigan, is perched in a dramatic position on a high bluff above the River Teifi. Seen from the deep wooded gorge below - as it was for centuries by the coracle fishermen - it presents a spectacular sight, which inspired great landscape artists such as Turner and Richard Wilson. Equally, the views, which visitors can enjoy from its ruined towers, are magnificent. The castle, small by comparison with Pembroke and the great Norman fortresses of North Wales, is mainly 13th century but despite its apparently unassailable position, it changed hands many times between the 12th and 14th centuries. Taken from the Normans by Lord Rhys in 1164, it was recaptured in 1204 by William Marshall; used as a base by Llewllyn the Great in 1215, when he summoned a Council of all Wales at Aberystwyth; taken again by the Normans in 1223, following which the present towers were built. After a period of decline and then refortification in the 14th century, the castle was captured again for a brief period by the Welsh in 1405 during the uprising of Owain Glyndwr.

Manorbier Castle

Haverfordwest Castle

Pembroke
Castle

NARBERTH CASTLE

Narberth Castle was built in the 13th Century. Its most notable Castellan being Sir Rhys ap Thomas who was given the castle by Henry VIII. By the 17th Century the castle had fallen into ruins, the remnants of which can be seen today and is now open to the public

NEVERN CASTLE

Very little remains of the castle but it provides an interesting view of the siting and layout of early medieval fortifications.

NEWPORT CASTLE

Newport Castle is another that is in private ownership and not open to the public.

PEMBROKE CASTLE

Pembroke Castle is one of the best preserved medieval castles in Wales. Open to visitors all year round, it is an intriguing place to explore. The wide walls are honeycombed with a seemingly endless system of rooms, passageways and spiralling flights of narrow stone steps; interpretative displays and information panels give a fascinating insight into the castle's origins and long history. One of the most impressive features is the distinctive round keep, which was built soon after 1200.

**tel: 01646 681510
or 684585
see advert page 41**

PICTON CASTLE

Picton Castle is privately owned and opened to the public six days a week. The beautifully laid out 40 acres of woodland gardens are well worth a visit. The castle lies three miles east of Haverfordwest.

tel: 01437 751326

ROCH CASTLE

Roch Castle is also a private residence. It is situated on the A487 from Haverfordwest.

Picton Castle

Castell Henllys

WISTON CASTLE

Although very little remains, the castle is worth a visit if only to see the remains of the shell keep built to help protect the motte and bailey castle. Owned by CADW, it be reached from Haverfordwest by taking the A40 towards Carmarthen and turning off at Wiston.

tel: 01443 336000

CARREG SAMSON

Situated in the coastal village of Abercastle, Carreg Samson is a Neolithic Cromlech overlooking the picturesque fishing village. To get there follow the A487 St. Davids road from Fishguard and then the signs to Abercastle.

CASTELL HENLLYS

Castell Henllys is the site of an Iron Age Fort, which has been recreated using authentic materials and techniques. To get there take the A487 from Fishguard to Cardigan, and look for the signs.

Narberth Castle

HAVERFORDWEST MUSEUM

Haverfordwest Town Museum is situated in the castle an overlooking the town and has been created to illustrate the history of the area. It houses exhibits explaining the castle and prison, which were once housed there, and the transport and industry into the town together with the institutions and personalities that make up Haverfordwest.

tel: 01437 763087
see advert page 75

LAMPHEY BISHOP'S PALACE

Lamphey Bishop's Palace has been acquired by CADW who have carried out careful renovation work to give visitors a rich insight into what the building looked like in a bygone age.

tel: 01443 336000

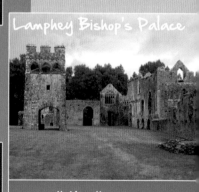

Lamphey Bishop's Palace

Castell Henllys

MILFORD HAVEN MUSEUM

The museum brings to life the fascinating story of the historic waterway and the new town's struggle to fulfil its potential. The Milford Haven story is a cycle of hopes dashed and dreams fulfilled and covers its brief period as a whaling port, which ended when gas replaced whale oil for lighting the streets of London. It also covers the town's attempts to become a great Trans-Atlantic port which floundered when the Great Western Railway terminus was built at Neyland and not Milford.

tel: 01646 694496
see advert page 84

PENRHOS COTTAGE

This is a typical North Pembrokeshire thatched cottage that has survived almost unchanged since the 19th Century. Built as an overnight cottage in about 1800 and later rebuilt in stone, Penrhos, with its original Welsh oak furniture, provides a unique opportunity to view the cottage's life in the past. The cottage is open by appointment.

**For further information contact Scolton Manor Museum
tel: 01437 731328**

PENTRE IFAN

Pentre Ifan is a Neolithic burial chamber dating back from around 3000BC. Administered by CADW, it can be reached via the A487 from Newport, then follow the signs for Pentre Ifan.

tel: 01443 336000

ST. DAVIDS BISHOP'S PALACE

Standing in the shadow of St. Davids Cathedral are the remains of the Bishop's Palace that was destroyed during the 16th Century. However much still remains to enable visitors to appreciate the scale of the imposing building.

tel: 01437 720517

Pentre Ifan

Bishop's Palace St. Davids

197

Tenby Museum

SCOLTON MANOR

A traditional Victorian country house, Scolton Manor was completed in 1842 and, until it was bought by Pembrokeshire County Council in 1972, was home to successive generations of the Higgon family. The Manor House has been sympathetically restored by the Museum Service in order to provide visitors with a taste of Victorian society and style, both above and below stairs. The 60 acres of park and woodland surrounding Scolton Manor are used as a country park. For children, there's a great recreational area towards the bottom of the park, including a wooden adventure play area, swings and slide – plus picnic tables for mum and dad to have a sit in the sun!

TENBY MUSEUM & ART GALLERY

Established in 1878, this national award winning museum is set in the ruins of a medieval castle. Exhibitions of local geology, local archaeology, maritime history, natural history and a social history exhibition called "The Story of Tenby". Events programme include talks, workshops and lectures for children and adults. Museum shop with books, cards, souvenirs and giftware. The Museum and Art Galley is open throughout the year.

**for all details
tel: 01834 842809
see advert page 21**

GARDENS

South West Wales enjoys some of the most beautiful gardens in the country. In this section we will take you through some of the places that are well worth a visit, offering stunning views and settings throughout Pembrokeshire, Ceredigion & Carmarthenshire, all of which are a short and easy drive away.

GARDENS

Picton Gardens

National Botanic Gardens

BRO MEIGAN GARDENS
Boncath
tel: 01239 841232

Inspirational gardens with a huge range of planting and a tearoom.

COLBY WOODLAND GARDENS
Nr Amroth
tel: 01834 811885

Eight acres of woodland garden set in a tranquil and secluded valley. Gift shop, tearooms, gallery and picnic area. Managed by The National Trust.

MANOROWEN WALLED GARDENS
Fishguard
tel: 01348 872168

Walled garden dating back to 1750. Semi-permanent exhibition of sculpture. Picnic area, teas and plants for sale.

MOORLAND COTTAGE PLANTS
Rhyd y Groes,
Brynberian, Crymych
tel: 01239 891363

Small country garden with themed areas. Open for charity and with panoramic views of the Preseil Mountains.

NEWBRIDGE NURSERY
Crundale, Nr Haverfordwest
tel: 01437 731678

A small family run nursery where visitors are welcome to enjoy the adjacent gardens including a wildlife meadow, water and bog garden and a riverside walk.

PENLAN UCHAF GARDENS
Gwaun Valley, Fishguard
tel: 01348 881388

Three acres of landscaped gardens set in the beautiful Gwaun Valley.

PICTON CASTLE
Rhos, Haverfordwest
tel: 01437 751326

40 acres of woodland and walled gardens with a unique collection.unusual shrubs, wild flowers, fern walk, fernery, maze, restored dewpond and herb collection. Spring and Autumn plant sales.

PENRALLT GARDEN CENTRE
Moylegrove, Nr Cardigan
tel: 01239 881295

Set in a beautiful location overlooking the sea and coast path above Ceibwr Bay, with a large and comprehensive collection of home grown and unusual plants.

PATIO & GARDEN
Wiston, Haverfordwest
tel: 01437 751343

An extensive range of pots, statues and sundials for patio and garden.

SCOLTON MANOR
Haverfordwest
tel: 01437 731328

Victorian Manor House, Museum and award winning Visitor Centre set in 60 acres of country park and woodlands.

HILTON COURT GARDENS & CRAFTS
Roch, Haverfordwest
tel: 01437 710262

8 acres of woodland gardens, island beds and borders containing a wide variety of unusual plants. Expanses of water and ponds, wild areas, a stream and waterfalls all add to the interest of this unique garden.

Upton Castle Chapel

Hilton Court

201

We are open every day, apart from Christmas Day.

April - September 10am - 6pm

October - March Hours 10am - 4.30pm

Fax: 01558 668933
Tel: 01558 668768
Email:
info@gardenofwales.org.uk

Admission Prices
Adults - £8.50
Concessions - £7.00
Children - £4.50
Under 5s - Free
Family (2 adults, 4 children) £21.00

The National Botanic Garden of Wales was the first botanic garden to open in the 21st century and the first to be created in the UK in nearly 200 years. With a collection of rare and endangered plant species from around the world, it stretches over 500 acres of beautiful, virtually pollution free countryside, across the site of a Regency parkland. Its gardens, lakes, woodlands, undulating hills and organically farmed meadows provide a harmonious blending of the natural and the cultivated. This constantly evolving young garden offers a range of year round attractions to appeal to the broadest interests. The centrepiece is the Great Glasshouse, the largest single span glasshouse in the world. Created by Lord Norman Foster, it houses a stunning display of mediterranean plants from across the globe.In 2007 a stunning Tropical House designed by John Belle was opened in the historic Double Walled Garden. The story of the evolution of flowering plants is told within the enchanting Double Walled Garden; the colourful Broadwalk is one of the longest herbaceous borders in Europe; modern water sculptures complement 200 year old water features and there are also dedicated Japanese, Marsh, Auricula, Bee, Apothecary, Wild, Genetic, Welsh Rare Plant and Slate Gardens. In our unique Edwardian Apothecaries Hall, exhibitions tell the story of the Physicians of Myddfai and Wales's unique knowledge of the links between plants and medicine. We warmly welcome visitors of all ages. Youngsters can scramble around our Adventure Play Zone and enjoy learning about plants in our exciting 360 degrees cinema. Visitors preferring a gentler pace can enjoy a buggy ride and guided tour; browse around our plant sales shop, or daydream beside the beautiful lakes. If you have access to the internet look us up on www.gardenofwales.org.uk to find out about our exciting programme of events and courses.

Gardd Fotaneg Genedlaethol Cymru

Mae'r Ardd ar agor gydol y flwyddyn ac yn cynnig diwrnod allan arbennig i'r teulu i gyd. Dewch i weld y Tŷ Gwydr un haen mwyaf yn y byd, a nifer o atyniadau eraill gan gynnwys:

- Tŷ Gwydr Mawr
- Tŷ Gwydr Trofannol Newydd
- Yr Ardd Japaneaidd
- Gardd Wenyn
- Oriel y Stablau
- Canolfan Ymwelwyr a Siop Rhoddion
- Theatr Botanica
- Planhigion i Lachau Exhibition
- Lle Chwarae i Blant
- Gwarchodfa Natur Genedlaethol Waun Las

National Botanic Garden of Wales

Open all year, the Garden offers a great day out for all the family. See the world's largest single span glass house and the many varied attractions including:

- Great Glasshouse
- Tropical House
- Japanese Garden
- Bee Garden
- Stables Gallery
- Gift Shop & Visitor Centre
- Theatr Botanica
- Plants for Health Exhibition
- Children's Play Area
- Waun Las National Nature Reserve

Rydym ar agor bob dydd ac eithrio Dydd Nadilig
Haf: 10am - 6pm
Gaeaf: 10am - 4.30pm

Open every day except Christmas Day
Summer: 10am - 6pm
Winter: 10am - 4.30pm

Mae cyfleusterau cynadleddo ac arlwyo ar gael ar gyfer hyd at 400 o bobl. Addas iawn ar gyfer ymweliadau ysgol.

I gaelprisiau a rhagor o wybodaeth cysylltwch â :
Gardd Fotaneg Genedlaethol Cymru, Llanarthne, Sir Gaerfyrddin SA32 8HG

National Botanic Garden of Wales
Gardd Fotaneg Genedlaethol Cymru

Conference and catering facilities for up to 400 people available. School visits highly recommended.

For prices and further information contact :
The National Botanic Garden of Wales, Llanarthne, Carmarthenshire SA32 8HG

01558 668768
www.gardenofwales.org.uk

LOTTERY FUNDED

Visit Wales National Tourism Awards 2007 - UK's favourite Lottery-funded Environment Project

ABERGLASNEY GARDENS

Aberglasney is one of the finest gardens in Wales and has been described as 'the Bodnant of the South'. The restoration of the house and garden started in 1997 and opened to the public in July 1999. Within the ten acres of garden there are three walled gardens and woodland walks, which contain a magnificent collection of plants, many of which are rarely seen in other gardens such as hardy orchids, Magnolias Trilliums and Meconopsis. The garden has been intentionally been planted to be of interest throughout the year.

At its heart is a unique and fully restored Elizabethan /Jacobean cloister and parapet walk, giving wonderful views over the Gardens and is the only example of this style of garden feature left in the U.K. The design of the Cloister Garden took into account the extensive archaeo-logical survey that was carried out on the site during 1999. This survey discovered some of the earliest garden features such as retaining walls and flights of steps, which date back to the late 16th century. Various older artefacts were also discovered including a silver Long Cross Penny dating back to

Edward Ic1282-1289 and a silver half groat dating back to Henry VII c1485-1509.

In 2005 a unique garden called the Ninfarium was created within the ruinous central rooms and courtyard of the mansion. The remaining walls of the rooms were stabilized and the entire area was covered with a huge glass atrium. This area now contains a fantastic collection of warm temperate and sub-tropical plants including Orchids, Palms, Magnolias and Cycads. In 2006 the Ninfarium won an award for the best garden design/construction project in the UK.

There is a Café in the grounds, which serves delectable light lunches and snacks. In the summer, tea can be taken on the terrace overlooking the Pool Garden. There is also a shop and plant sales area. The Garden and Café at Aberglasney are open every day, (except Christmas Day).

**Llangathen,
Carmarthenshire
Tel: 01558 668998**
see advert page 231

DAY TOURS BY CAR IN PEMBROKESHIRE

For those visitors who like to explore by car, these seven day drives will show you much of Pembrokeshire's varied landscape. The routes suggested, cover the south, west, north and central regions of the county, and each tour brings you back to your original starting point. All are intended as a leisurely drive with plenty of interesting features along the way.

TOUR 1
TENBY - CAREW - LLAWHADEN - NARBERTH - AMROTH - SAUNDERSFOOT - TENBY

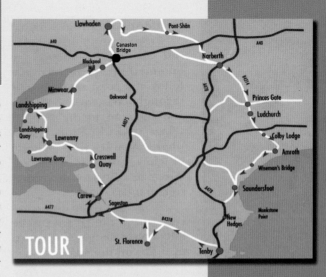

TOUR 1

From Tenby take the B4318 to St. Florence where you can take in the magnificent views across the Ritec Valley. After Manor House Leisure Park, turn left to the pretty village of St. Florence, which features a Flemish style chimney. Leave St. Florence and return to the B4318, turning left for Sageston. At Sageston follow the A477 towards Pembroke for three quarters of a mile then turn right off of the roundabout onto the A4075 for Carew, which has its own castle, Celtic cross and 17th century bridge. Turn left after the bridge for free car parking. After leaving Carew proceed up the hill, turn left on the minor road to Cresswell Quay where the estuary is frequented by herons and kingfishers. Then its on to Lawrenny where at the quay there are yachting facilities, pleasant riverside walks, a picnic site and the fantastic Lawrenny Quay Tearooms. Landshipping Quay, the next village you arrive at, offers a tranquil setting with riverside views. From here follow the signs for Minwear and then on to Blackpool Mill where there is a restored mill, cafe and riverside and woodland walks.

Take the A4075 down the hill to the A40 at Canaston Bridge, then take the second exit at the roundabout signposted Llawhaden where there is a castle and beautiful parish church. Left over the village bridge takes you to Pont-Shan where turning right onto the B4314 takes you to the market town of Narberth. Leave Narberth on the B4314 for Princes Gate, go straight on the crossroads heading for Ludchurch and follow the road for Longstone, go straight over the next crossroads for Colby Lodge which features National Trust property and gardens. From Colby Lodge proceed up the hill to the T -junction and turn right for Amroth, an unspoilt coastal village with shops, pubs, restaurants,

Saundersfoot

207

Tenby

superb beach at low tide and seafront parking. From Amroth drive up the hill to the Junction at Summerhill, turn left and follow the coast road, passing through Wiseman's Bridge and then on to the popular village resort of Saundersfoot, where you will find superb beaches, tunnel walks to Wiseman's Bridge, shops and restaurants. From Saundersfoot proceed out of the village to New Hedges and return to Tenby on the A478.

TOUR 2
TENBY - LYDSTEP - MANORBIER - LAMPHEY - FRESHWATER EAST STACKPOLE - PEMBROKE - CAREW -TENBY

Leave Tenby on the A4139 signposted Pembroke and as you approach Lydstep village note the pull in on the left hand side of the road giving superb views of Caldey

Island and the cliffs towards Giltar Point. After passing through Lydstep village, turn left at the crossroads to Manorbier, B4585. For a detour to one of the best beaches in Pembrokeshire, follow the signs to Shrinkle Haven where you'll find good parking. Retrace your steps back to the B4585 and turn left to Manorbier village where there is a Norman castle and church, village shops, pub, cafe and beach. Leave Manorbier on the B4585 signposted Pembroke and rejoin the A4139, which takes you through Jameston and Hodgeston and on to Lamphey where there is a ruined medieval Bishop's Palace.From Lamphey rejoin the B4584 to Freshwater East where there is a beach, sand dunes and access to the coastal path. To reach Stackpole Quay cross the narrow bridge by the beach and follow the road through East Trewent for about two miles where you will find a small harbour. large car park and coast path to Barafundle

Manorbier

beach. Return to the T-junction and turn left to the village of Stackpole, following the road through National Trust woodland to the B4319. Turn right for Pembroke where there is a magnificent medieval castle and tourist information centre. To return to Tenby, leave Pembroke along main street and follow the signpost for St. Clears. At the major junction with the A477, turn right and after about two miles on the A4075 at the roundabout for Carew, where there is another medieval castle and a Celtic cross, tidal mill, walks, pub and riverside picnic area. Return to the A477 and turn left. Turn right off of the roundabout onto the B4318 signposted Tenby and follow all the way into Tenby.

wildlife, access to Broad Haven beach, pub and tearooms. Continue through Bosherston, turning left for Broad Haven where there is a large clifftop car park, outstanding views and a superb beach. Re-trace the road back to Bosherston, turning left in the village for St. Govans Head which has a remarkable chapel in the cliffs and spectacular views over dramatic coastal features such as Huntsman's Leap. Back through Bosherston to the B4319 turn left for Castlemartin. After you pass Merrion Camp, where two tanks are on display at the entrance, turn left for Stack Rocks. The road passes medieval Flimston Chapel and leads to a large clifftop car park. Stack Rocks, two vertical columns that are home to thousands of breeding seabirds in early summer,

Pembroke Castle

TOUR 3

PEMBROKE - BOSHERSTON - T. GOVANS - STACK ROCKS - CASTLEMARTIN - FRESHWATER WEST - ANGLE - PEMBROKE

From Pembroke take the B4319 for Bosherston. After about 3 miles note St. Petrox Church on your right. Continue, turning left at the signpost for Bosherston, where there are lily ponds, a church, fishing, superb walks,

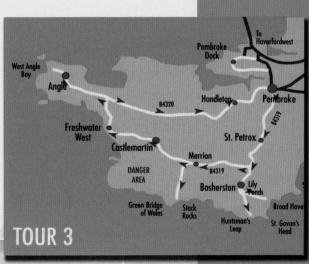

Bosherston

Freshwater West

209

Dale

stand just offshore a few hundred yards to your left. A short distance to your right is a viewing platform for the Green Bridge of Wales, a spectacular limestone arch. Return to the B4319 and turn left for Castlemartin where an 18th century circular stone cattle pound is now a traffic round-about. Fork left for Freshwater West, noted for its long wide beach backed by rolling sand dunes, with a restored beach hut once used for drying seaweed to make laverbread. Continue along the coast road, which gives more superb views as it climbs again towards a T-junction. Turn left here on the B4320 for Angle , passing the huge Texaco refinery and views across the estuary towards Milford Haven and the busy shipping lanes. In the old

fishing village of Angle, which lies between East Angle Bay and West Angle Bay, interesting sights include the church and the remains of the medieval Tower House. West Angle Bay has a beach, cafe, parking, together with views of Thorn Island and the Haven, whilst East Angle Bay is home to a lifeboat station, yacht moorings, outstanding views and walks. Return to Pembroke on the B4320 via Hundleton.

TOUR 4

HAVERFORDWEST - MILFORD HAVEN - DALE - MARLOES - LITTLE HAVEN - BROAD HAVEN - NOLTON HAVEN - NEWGALE - HAVERFORDWEST

Leave Haverfordwest on the A4076, passing through Johnston towards Milford Haven, which offers easy parking at both the Rath and the marina. Attractions here include a museum, adventure playground, choice of eateries, boat trips and pleasant walks and views along the Haven waterway. From Milford Haven follow the road signposted Herbrandston and

TOUR 4

Map labels: Newgale, Roch, Simpson Cross, Nolton, Nolton Cross, Druidston, Haroldston, Stack Rocks, Broad Haven, Little Haven, Haverfordwest, St. Bride's, Talbenny, Skomer Island, Martin's Haven, Musselwick Sands, Marloes, Marloes Sands, Skokholm Island, West Dale Beach, Dale, Dale Point, Johnston, Herbrandston, Milford Haven, St. Ann's Head, Angle, Pembroke Dock

Marloes

Broad Haven

210

Dale, eventually joining the B4327 from Haverfordwest about two and a half miles from Dale which is a mecca for watersports enthusiasts. Then its on to St. Ann's Head which features a lighthouse, together with out standing views of the Atlantic and the entrance to the Haven waterway. Retrace your journey to Dale from where you can take a detour to West Dale Beach by turning left by the church and leaving your car at the end of the road. After Dale take the B4327 for about one and a half miles and turn left to Marloes where you will discover one of Pembrokeshire's most beautiful beaches at Marloes Sands. Martins Haven is well worth a visit for here the coast road culminates in a National Trust car park, and a walk from Martin's Haven to the headland will give you outstanding views of Skomer, Skokholm and St. Bride's Bay. Return to Marloes and follow the signs for Dale, turning left at the T-junction. After about a quarter of a mile turn left for St. Bride's. Your next port of call is the small, pretty seaside village of Little Haven, which is accessible via various country lanes that take you through Talbenny. From Little Haven follow the road to Broad Haven, where there is easy parking and a haven for watersport enthusiasts featuring a long beach, outstanding views and walks, interesting rock formations,

shops and other facilities. From Broad Haven take the coast road north for Nolton Haven, which takes you on to Newgale another long beach offering watersports and views towards nearby St. Davids, From Newgale take the A487 to Haverfordwest returning via Roch and Simpson Cross.

Fishguard

TOUR 5

HAVERFORDWEST -
CLARBESTON ROAD -
LLYS-Y-FRAN - MAENCLOCHOG -
ROSEBUSH GWAUN VALLEY -
DINAS CROSS - FISHGUARD -
STRUMBLE HEAD - MATHRY
LETTERSTON - TREFFGARNE
GORGE - HAVERFORDWEST

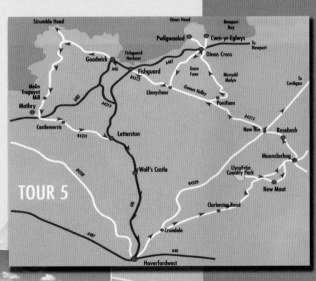

TOUR 5

Haverfordwest

Llys-y-Fran

211

Pwllgwaelod

Leave Haverfordwest on the Withybush and Crundale road, the B4329, turning right on the minor road signposted Clarbeston Road and Llys-y-Fran. Carefully follow the signs for Llys-y-Fran Country Park, where there is a reservoir used for fishing and a visitor centre and restaurant. From the country park rejoin the road to nearby Gwastad where a short detour to New Moat is well worthwhile. Return to the Gwastad road and go on to the pretty village of Maenclochog. Follow the B4313 to Rosebush, a village whose claim to fame is that slates from its quarries were used to roof the House of Parliament, and continue to the crossroads at New Inn. Here you turn right and climb to one of the highest points of the Preseli Hills, which offer superb views. Return to the crossroads at New Inn, turning right on the B4313 for Fishguard.Continue along the B4313 for about 5 miles and turn left down the hill for Pontfaen. After the village bridge go straight on at the crossroads and up the very steep hill for Dinas Cross. This moorland road gives outstanding views across Newport Bay before descending to Dinas Cross. At the T-junction turn right onto the A487 and turn immediately left for Pwllgwaelod. Return to the A487, turn left and then go to left again for Cwm-yr-Eglwys, a picturesque beach famed for a ruined church. Retrace your steps back to the main road where you turn right for Fishguard. Follow the road for about 2 miles then turn left to Llanychaer. This road is very narrow and steep in places. After passing over the bridge in the village rejoin the B4313, turning right for Fishguard, home of the Rosslare to Fishguard Ferry Terminal, passing through picturesque Lower Fishguard, a popular film location. At the roundabout by the Stena Line terminal, proceed up the hill and follow the signs for Strumble Head where there is a lighthouse and spectacular views of the coastline. Retracing your steps follow the coast road towards Mathry, which features an unusual parish church, stunning views and an ancient burial site nearby. From there follow the signs for Letterston where you turn right at the crossroads in the village onto the A40 and head back to Haverfordwest via Treffgarne Gorge which offers striking rock formations and spectacular views.

Cwm-yr-Eglwys

St Davids

Newgale

Solva

TOUR 6

TOUR 6
HAVERFORDWEST - NEWGALE - SOLVA MIDDLE MILL - ST. DAVIDS - ABEREIDDY - PORTHGAIN - ABERCASTLE - TREFIN - HAVERFORDWEST

Take the A487 out of Haverfordwest signposted St. Davids passing through Simpson Cross and Roch, on to Newgale which offers superb views over St. Bride's Bay. Next stop is Solva where there is a beautiful natural harbour, pretty village, shops and excellent walks. Continuing on this road brings you to the tiny city of St. Davids, which boasts a cathedral, Bishop's Palace, shops, restaurants, art galleries and outdoor activities, together with an information centre. From St. Davids you can take the minor road to Porth Clais, another picturesque little harbour, and St. Justinian, where there is a RNLI lifeboat station and views across Ramsey Sound.

Returning to St. Davids follow the signs to Fishguard for a short distance before turning left for Whitesands Bay. Here you will find one of the finest beaches in Britain and many other watersport activities. Return towards the A487 follow the signs for Abereiddy where adjacent to the pebble beach is the Blue Lagoon. From

Abereiddy

213

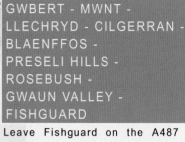

DAY TOURS BY CAR IN PEMBROKESHIRE

Abereiddy, take the coast road to Llanrhian and turn left for Porthgain which has a history of exporting slate across the world. Returning to Llanrhian turn left at the crossroads for Trefin where there is a youth hostel, partly restored mill, hand weaving centre, gallery and craft shop. The next harbour along this rugged coastline is Abercastle, home to the Carreg Samson burial chamber. Follow the road out of Abercastle for the village of Mathry which brings you back to the B4331 to Letterston where you turn right onto the A40 and on to Haverforwest via Treffgarne Gorge.

Newport Sands

Fishguard

TOUR 7

FISHGUARD - DINAS CROSS - NEWPORT - NEVERN - MOYLEGROVE - POPPIT SANDS - ST. DOGMAELS - CARDIGAN -

GWBERT - MWNT - LLECHRYD - CILGERRAN - BLAENFFOS - PRESELI HILLS - ROSEBUSH - GWAUN VALLEY - FISHGUARD

Leave Fishguard on the A487 towards Cardigan. Continue to Newport and Nevern where there is a Celtic Cross and Pilgrims Cross. En route two detours are recommended. The first is to one of Britain's best prehistoric burial chambers, Pentre Ifan, which can be found by turning right off the A487 before the Nevern turnoff and following the narrow country lanes to the top of the hill. The second detour is to Castell Henllys, a reconstructed Iron Age Fort managed by the National Park Authority. After Nevern proceed on the B4582 and take the third left hand

TOUR 7

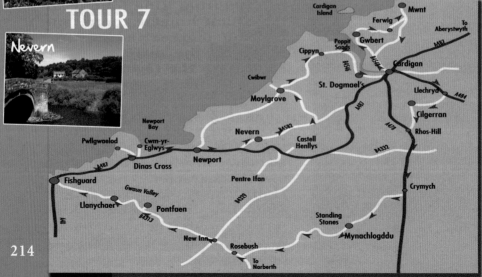

Nevern

214

St Dogmaels

Mwnt Church

Poppit Sands

Pentre Ifan

turn signposted Moylegrove, an attractive coastal village dating back to Norman times. In the village turn left along the narrow road to the pebble beach at Ceibwr Bay. From Moylegrove follow the narrow country lanes to Poppit Sands, a large sandy beach with car park and lifeboat station, together with views of the Teifi estuary. Close to Poppit Sands is St. Dogmael's, an attractive hillside village that features the ruins of a 12th century Benedictine abbey and parish church containing the Sagranus Stone. From St. Dogmael's the road takes you over the bridge to the historic market town of Cardigan and along the northern bank of the River Teifi to Gwbert and then Mwnt. Returning to Cardigan take the A484 to Llechryd and Cilgerran, home to coracles on the Teifi and the Welsh Wildlife Centre. From Cilgerran drive to Rhos-Hill where you join the A478 and the village of Crymych. On leaving the village, go through Mynachlogddu along a country road that takes you through the heart of the Preseli Hills. Return towards the village and follow the signpost for Rosebush. Continue to the cross roads at New Inn and go straight on for Fishguard where the road takes you alongside the beautiful Gwuan Valley, and offers detours to the villages of Pontfaen and Llanychaer.

CEREDIGION & CARDIGAN BAY

Just across the Teifi estuary from Poppit Sands and St. Dogmaels is the ancient county of Cardiganshire, or Ceredigion as it is now known in Welsh. Like Pembrokeshire, it is a county with a rich and varied landscape together with a long and dramatic history and it is well known to countless holidaymakers as the home of such popular resorts as New Quay, Aberaeron and Aberystwyth. Its spectacular coastline is marked by many fine beaches

CEREDIGION

Aberaeron

Aberporth

Aberystwyth

EXPLORING CEREDIGION

Historic Cardigan, which received its first Royal Charter in 1199 from King John, is an important holiday centre and thriving market town and is one of the main shopping centres for the region. Beautifully sited near the mouth of the River Teifi with some of Wales' most attractive coast and countryside right on the doorstep, its shops and narrow streets retain the town's character. The Market Hall, built in 1859 and featuring impressive stone arches, holds a general market twice weekly and a livestock market once a week. Visitor attractions include the Theatr Mwldan (housed in the same building as the Tourist Information Centre - both of which are open all year round), an indoor leisure centre, a golf club at nearby Gwbert and a large annual arts festival, Gwyl Fawr Aberteifi. Crossing the Teifi below the castle is the striking multi-arched stone bridge. Sources disagree as to whether this is the original Norman Bridge, strengthened and widened in later years, or whether it was constructed in the 17th or even 18th century. The history of Cardigan Castle raises less argument. The ruins that now remain date from 1240, and it must have been in an earlier castle that the very first National Eisteddfod - advertised for a whole year beforehand throughout Wales, England and Scotland, was hosted by Rhys ap Gruffudd in 1176. The National

217

Aberaeron

New Quay

Eisteddfod is now the major cultural event in the Welsh calendar, as well as being Europe's largest peripatetic cultural festival. Cardigan Castle, like so many others, was destroyed by Cromwell, and now all that remains is privately owned. More recently, Cardigan was one of Wales' most prominent ports having as many as 300 ships registered there. Shipbuilding thrived in the 19th century when the busy warehouses along the waterfront handled everything from exports of herring, corn, butter and slate to imports of limestone, salt, coal, timber for shipbuilding, and manufactured goods. Human cargo was carried too: emigrant ships sailed from Cardigan to New York in the USA and New Brunswick in Canada. This prosperous period for Cardigan was relatively short-lived. Inevitably booming trade meant that ships were getting bigger all the time while the gradual silting of the estuary was making access to Cardigan more and more restricted. The final nail in the town's coffin as a commercial port was the coming of the railway in 1885 - but today, as a popular holiday destination, Cardigan is once again a busy centre of attention, boasting many attractions within easy reach. Several of these stand near the banks of the Teifi such as St Dogmael's Abbey, Poppit Sands, the Welsh Wildlife Centre, Cilgerran Castle and Cenarth Falls.

FELINWYNT RAINFOREST CENTRE

Visit this mini-rainforest and experience a different world. Wander amongst exotic plants and tropical butterflies accompanied by the sounds of the Peruvian Amazon. Waterfalls and streams enhance the humidity and someone is on hand to explain the mysteries of butterflies and to answer any questions. Watch the fascinating Leaf Cutter Ants. The visitor centre comprises the nature gift shop and an excellent cafe serving meals and snacks all day (why not try one of Dorothy's homemade cakes). The centre is suitable for the disabled.

Crayons and paper are provided free for children to create pictures for display in the gallery. The centre can be found 6 miles from Cardigan and 4 miles from Aberporth; follow the brown signs from the A487 at Blanannerch.

**for more information ring
01239 810250
or 810882**

TALYLLYN RAILWAY WHARF STATION TYWYN

The main station of the narrow gauge Talyllyn Railway is at Tywyn on the mid-Wales coast. From there, the line runs inland for over seven miles to Nant Gwernol, most of the route being in Snowdonia National Park. Built in 1865 to bring slate to the coast, the Railway was taken over by the Talyllyn Railway Preservation Society in 1951, becoming the first pre-served railway in the world. The railway operates on some days in February and March, daily from 2nd April to 30th October, and at Christmas. All passenger trains are hauled by coal fired steam locomotives. Tywyn Wharf station has a shop and restaurant, as well as The Narrow Gauge Railway Museum with exhibits from over 70 railways.

Talyllyn Railway

Talyllyn Railway

Talyllyn Railway

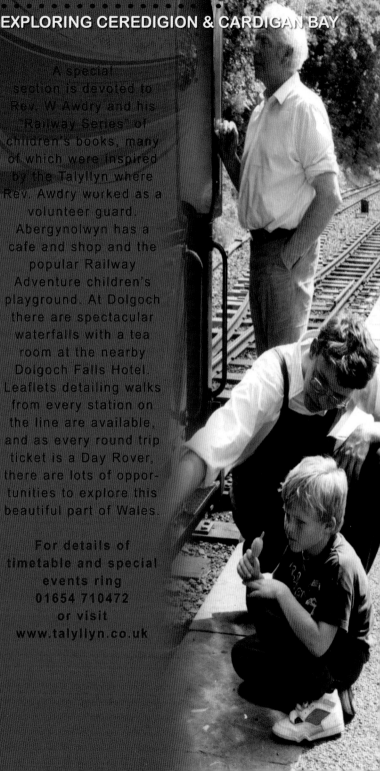

A special section is devoted to Rev. W Awdry and his "Railway Series" of children's books, many of which were inspired by the Talyllyn where Rev. Awdry worked as a volunteer guard. Abergynolwyn has a cafe and shop and the popular Railway Adventure children's playground. At Dolgoch there are spectacular waterfalls with a tea room at the nearby Dolgoch Falls Hotel. Leaflets detailing walks from every station on the line are available, and as every round trip ticket is a Day Rover, there are lots of opportunities to explore this beautiful part of Wales.

For details of timetable and special events ring
01654 710472
or visit
www.talyllyn.co.uk

CANOLFANNAU CROESO CEREDIGION
TOURIST INFORMATION CENTRES

ABERYSTWYTH TIC
Terrace Road
Aberystwyth
SY23 2AG
01970 612125
aberystwythtic@ceredigion.gov.uk

ABERAERON TIC
The Quay
Aberaeron
SA46 0BT
01545 570602
aberaerontic@ceredigion.gov.uk

CARDIGAN TIC
Theatr Mwldan
Cardigan
SA43 2JY
01239 613230
cardigantic@ceredigion.gov.uk

EASTER – SEPTEMBER

BORTH TIC
High Street
Borth
SY24 5HY
01970 871174
borthtic@ceredigion.gov.uk

NEW QUAY TIC
Church Street
New Quay
SA45 9NZ
01545 560865
NewQuayTIC@ceredigion.gov.uk

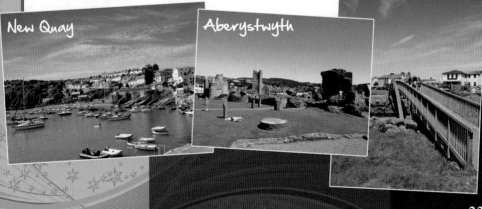

New Quay

Aberystwyth

Aberaeron

VALE OF RHEIDOL RAILWAY
Aberystwyth

An unforgettable journey through the spectacular Rheidol Valley by narrow gauge steam train on one of the "Great Little Trains of Wales". The journey between Aberystwyth and Devil's Bridge takes about an hour in each direction and the train overcomes a height difference of 600ft giving superb views of the Rheidol Valley. The Railway which opened in 1902 to serve the lead mining industry, was the last steam train railway owned by British Rail. It has undergone major renovation with improvement work continuing. Trains depart from the centre of Aberystwyth adjacent to the British Rail station. Ample parking is available in their car parks off Park Avenue and at Devil's Bridge.

**TRAINS RUN MOST DAYS
EASTER - OCT
TEL: 01970 625819**

CARMARTHENSHIRE

Carmarthenshire is a very attractive holiday destination for visitors who appreciate history, culture and a green and beautiful environment. Covering an area of 1,000 square miles, the county is a veritable feast of delights and discovery. The 50 miles of stunning coastline embrace vast stretches of safe golden sands such as the beaches of Cefn Sidan and Pendine, punctuated by the Taf and Towy estuaries, which so inspired the legendary writer Dylan Thomas. The county is also rich in bustling market towns, such as Newcastle Emlyn, Llandysul, Whitland, Llandeilo, Llandovery and Llanybydder and of course Carmarthen.

CARMARTHEN

Carmarthen, the reputed birth-place of Merlin - wizard and counsellor to King Arthur. The town stands eight miles inland on the River Towy - a position that inspired the Romans to make it their strategic capital. They also built an amphitheatre here, rediscovered in 1936 but not excavated until 1968. Today Carmarthen's quaint old narrow streets are full of Welsh character and tradition. There's also a first-class modern shopping centre with its many familiar high street names, which expanded with the opening of a new shopping complex with cinema in 2010. In Carmarthen you're also likely to catch more than a smattering of Welsh, as it is still widely spoken here. It is believed that the oldest manu-script in the Welsh language - The Black Book of Carmarthen - now in the National Library of Wales in Aberystwyth - was written in the town. A few miles west is Derllys Court Golf Club, near Bancyfelin, which has an interesting 18 hole, pay as you play, set in a beautiful location amongst rolling countryside. There is a licensed bar together

Pendine

with catering facilities and a warm welcome is extended to visitors.

for more information ring 01267 211575

Another attraction virtually on Carmarthen's doorstep is the Gwili Railway at Bronwydd Arms (just off the A484) - one of Wales' last remaining standard gauge steam railways where a train takes you to a wooded riverside area deep in the valley where there is also a picnic site.

The railway opened in 1860 and eventually became the property of British Railways, but after the remaining milk traffic was transferred to road, the line closed in 1973. The Gwili Railway Company was set up in 1975 and in 1978, and thanks to volunteers a section of the line just over a mile long was reopened between the Bronwydd Arms and the riverside station at Llwyfan Cerrig. An extension towards Cynwyl Elfed is progressing well.

Cenarth

LAUGHARNE

An ancient and interesting township standing on the west bank of the Taf estuary. Originally a fortified Roman station, the township is thought to have been founded by the Princes of Dynevor prior to the Norman conquest. It has enjoyed several names over the centuries, Abercorran (at the mouth of the Corran) Tallachar, Thalacharne and modern day Laugharne. The town is dominated by the castle which was built in Norman times as part of a line of fortified garrisons along the Carmarthenshire and Pembrokeshire coast designed to keep the local inhabitants under control. It has had a varied history and played a prominent role in the Civil War when it withstood a Cromwellian siege for seven days. More recently, CADW spent twenty years carrying out sympathetic restoration work and it is now open to the public. Laugharne and Malmesbury in Wiltshire are the only towns in the UK to retain their ancient Charter, granted not by Parliament, but by Royal decree and which allows them to be governed by a Corporation in addition to the normal local government bodies.

Laugharne

Dylan Thomas Boathouse

Laugharne

The Corporation is headed by the Portreeve with a Foreman, a Recorder, two Common Attorneys, four Constables, a Baliff and a Jury consisting of twenty Burgesses. This august body of men meets on a monthly basis and many matters of local interest are discussed and decided upon. These sittings are held in the Town Hall where the original Charter is displayed together with many other articles of historic interest. Once every three years, the local population of Laugharne take part in the Common Walk when the boundaries of theTownship are walked and identified. This is a walk of some twenty six miles through very rough and difficult countryside and for those brave enough to take part, refreshments are served during the route. In more recent times Laugharne became the home of the famous Welsh poet Dylan Thomas and his well known work - Under Milk Wood - was undoubtedly inspired by the Township and its inhabitants. His home, The Boathouse, is now a museum to his life and works and is open to the public.

227

EXPLORING CARMARTHENSHIRE

From Laugharne, the road west cuts a picturesque route to Pendine Sands, where Sir Malcom Campbell and others made several attempts on the world landspeed record, the most recent being in 1998. The fatal crash of Parry Thomas-Jones in 1927 ended Pendine's racing career, but the exciting new Museum of Speed recalls this village resort's days of fame and glory. On the eastern side of Carmarthen Bay are the estuaries of the Gwendraeth and Loughor, and the superb seven mile beach of Cefn Sidan Sands - one of the best beaches in Britain.

WHITLAND

Whitland, which stands on the River Taf inside the Carmarthenshire border, west of St. Clears, rose in prominence as a market town in the 19th century. The coming of the railway established it as an important junction. The town's most significant place in history goes back to the 10th century, when the great Welsh king Hywel Dda (Hywel the Good) called an assembly of wise men here to draw up a unified legal code for Wales, based on the ancient tribal laws and customs already in existence. The assembly took place at Ty Gwyn ar Daf (The White House on the Taf) - Hywel Dda's hunting lodge. It is thought that the house could have been the site chosen two centuries later for Whitland Abbey. The Hywel Dda Interpretive Gardens and Centre, in the centre of the town, now commemorate this great assembly. Whitland Abbey was the first Cistercian monastery in Wales and gave rise to seven others, including Strata Florida which was founded in 1140, but unfortunately virtually nothing remains of the abbey today, its ruins standing to the north of Whitland.

Pendine

Cenarth

Botanic Gardens

LLANELLI

Once the tinplate capital of the world and arguably the home of Welsh rugby, Llanelli is a thriving town with an impressive pedestrianised shopping centre and bustling indoor and outdoor markets. Standing on the beautiful Loughor estuary, Llanelli has a pleasant beach and is close to many major attractions. These include the recently developed Millennium Coastal Park, Pembrey Country Park, magnificent Cefn Sidan Sands, the Pembrey Motorsports Centre and Kidwelly Castle. Places to visit include Parc Howard and Sandy Water Park.

CORACLE CENTRE & MILL, CENARTH

The strange, round fishing boat, known as the coracle, has been a familiar sight on the River Teifi for centuries. It is light, manoeuvrable and ideal in shallow water, though mastering the art of coracle fishing can take years of practice. Today there are still 12 pairs licensed to fish on the Teifi, but the best place to see coracles is the National Coracle Centre which houses over 20 different types of coracle, in varying shapes and sizes, from all over the world - India, Vietnam, Tibet, Iraq and North America - as well as 9 varieties of Welsh coracle and examples from England and Scotland. An added bonus for visitors is that in the workshop you can see how coracles are made. The Coracle Centre stands on the ground floor of a 17th century flourmill, which is also open to visitors, and there are arts, crafts, souvenirs and gifts for sale.

for more information
ring 01239 710980
or 710507

Cenarth

229

McDonald's ™

CARMARTHEN
MYRTLE HILL, PENSARN
TELEPHONE: **01267 220861**

OPEN 24HRS 7 DAYS A WEEK*

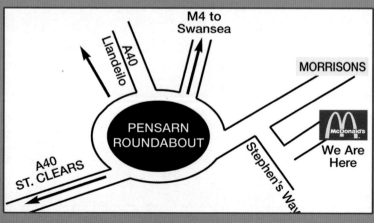

M4 to Swansea

A40 Llandeilo

MORRISONS

McDonald's
We Are Here

PENSARN ROUNDABOUT

A40 ST. CLEARS

Stephen's Way

*DRIVE THRU ONLY AFTER 11PM

CENARTH

MUSEUM OF THE WELSH WOOLLEN INDUSTRY
Drefach Velindre

Cenarth is one of the most popular beauty spots in the whole of West Wales. Standing on the River Teifi, it is a very pretty village, famous for its salmon leap falls. It is also recognised as the traditional home of the Teifi coracle, and here you will find the National Coracle Centre, which despite its name is a private enterprise, though no less important or interesting for that. Unspoilt Cenarth is a designated conservation area, with many of its buildings listed. The fine old bridge is believed to be 18th century, and the flourmill, which houses the Coracle Centre dates from the 1600's.

The new museum promises not only to do justice to the fascinating story of wool but also continue in commercial production, producing fabrics in traditional patterns and re-interpreting designs for a contemporary market. Imaginative displays, a new cafe and shop selling the very best of Welsh textiles are just some of the treats in store for visitors. The museum has facilities for the disabled and admission is free. Located 4 miles east of Newcastle Emlyn, 16 miles west of Carmarthen. Follow the brown tourist signs.

For more information ring 01559 370929

MCDONALDS (Carmarthen)

**MYRTLE HILL, PENSARN,
LLANGUNNOR, SA31 2NG
Tel: 01267 220861**

Excellent quality food for the family in a hurry.
Recently refurbished restaurant and with drive
thru facility.

**SEE ADVERT
PAGE 230**

CASTLE VIEW TAKE-AWAY & RESTAURANT

GRIST SQUARE, LAUGHARNE, Tel: 01994 427445

Traditional cooked fish and chips, using the very best
of ingredients, lots home made. Take away or eat in our
licensed restaurant.

Opening hours: Monday to Friday 12.00pm to 2.30pm
and 5.00pm to 8.30pm, Saturdays 12.00 to 8.30pm
Sunday (Easter to October
12.00pm to 7.00pm)

Closed on Thursdays

A TASTE OF CORNWALL

**36 BLUE STREET, CARMARTHEN,
Tel: 07929741120**

A large & varied menu of freshly baked
pasties including many vegetarian options.
Freshly prepared
baguettes and paninis with
hot or cold fillings.

SEE ADVERT PAGE 225

MCDONALDS (Swansea)

**PENLLERGAER, JUNCTION 47 M4
Tel: 01792 898655**

Excellent quality food for the
family in a hurry,
with drive thru facility.

**SEE ADVERT
PAGE 233**

SWANSEA

PENLLERGAER

JUNCTION 47 M4

TELEPHONE: 01792 898655

OPEN 5AM UNTIL 12AM SUNDAY – THURSDAY

FRI & SAT 24HRS*

NEW PLAY AREA

DRIVE THRU ONLY AFTER 11PM

SOUTH EAST IRELAND

Explore 10,000 years of Irish history in a day! Begin with the Irish National Heritage Park in Wexford and discover how the Irish lived from the Stone Age to the 12th century. Travel to Waterford and its fabulous Museum of Treasures, tracing the history of Ireland's most ancient city, before lunch in a centuries old pub. See how the world famous Waterford Crystal is made, then journey to the marvellous castles of Lismore and Cahir and then the magical Rock of Cashel before ending your day at Kilkenny Castle, dining at one of medieval Kilkenny's superb restaurants. A medieval fortress that has stood witness to many key moments in Irish history, a beautifully restored castle that has stood guard over a city for over 900 years... History you can touch and feel is all around in the south east region, an area linked by a network of five ancient river valleys and containing Ireland's oldest city, Waterford. Follow the trail of previous visitors, Celts, Vikings and Normans through magnificent castles and monuments, heritage museums and great country houses. Discover the creative heart of Ireland's traditional crafts and some of Europe's most beautiful gardens, cruise on Ireland's second largest river or enjoy game, sea and coarse angling in the cleaning of rivers and lakes or off miles of stunning coastline. Here's just a taste of what is in store: Follow the epic story of five generations of Kennedy's at the Ancestral Home of JF. Kennedy in Wexford. You can still see the original farmyard of the President's Great Grandfather. The John F Kennedy Arboterum in Wexford, dedicated to the memory of the late President, has over 4,000 individual species of trees from around the world. Follow the footsteps of the famine period emigrants on the Dunbrody Famine Ship in Wexford, a full scale reconstruction of a 19th famine ship. Learn the heroic tale of the 1798 rebellion in Ireland at the interactive displays at the award-winning National 1798 Visitor Centre in Wexford. Lismore Heritage Centre in Co Waterford, tells the fascinating story of the town's history from its Celtic origins onwards. Part of that story is the 17th century Lismore 13th century Hook Lighthouse in Wexford is the oldest working lighthouse in Northern Europe and now has a craft shop and restaurant.

Now fully restored to its former glory, as are its beautiful public gardens, Kilkenny Castle has stood guard over the lovely city of Kilkenny for over 900 years. Kilkenny is also known for atmospheric traditional pubs and fabulous restaurants, as well as for some of Ireland's finest craft producers. Most of these can be found at the world famous Kilkenny Design Centre, housed in the old castle stables.

County Kilkenny is also home to one of Ireland's finest monastic settlements, Jerpoint Abbey and the magical Dunmore Cave, whose underground chambers were formed over millions of years. You can also explore massive caverns at one of Europe's most famous show-caves, Mitchelstown Cave in Tipperary.

There's a mystical aura around the Rock Of Cashel in Tipperary, a spectacular settlement of medieval buildings, including a 12th century round tower, 13th century Gothic cathedral and 15th century castle. The Brú Ború Cultural Centre, adjoining it, offers a folk theatre, genealogy suite and underground theatre and an exhibition telling the story of Irish song and dance. Nearby, the Cashel Folk Village, a collection of thatched buildings recreates traditional Irish village life.

Castle Cahir, imposingly situated on a rocky island on the river Suir in Tipperary, is one of Ireland's largest and best preserved castles, with an impressive keep, tower and much of its defensive structure still intact. In Carlow, fascinating Huntingdon Castle and Gardens, rebuilt in 1625, boasts an ancient vine in its conservatory and a famous avenue of yew trees in its beautiful gardens. In Tipperary, famous Dungarvan Castle, an Anglo-Norman fortification, was built by King John in the 12th century.

IRISH FERRIES

How good are we? Ask any of our passengers.

Super Cruise Ferry to Ireland from Pembroke Dock

For Car & Passenger Reservations
Tel 08705 171717

IRISH FERRIES

Irish Ferries operate to Rosslare on the south east coast of Ireland with the luxury 34,000 ton cruise ferry, the m.v Isle of Inishmore. You have the choice of afternoon or early morning sailings and the crossing takes you down the Milford Haven Waterway and out past the 2 bird sanctuary islands of Skokholm and Skomer before heading across St Georges Channel to the Tusker Rock Lighthouse which is seen approximately half an hour before arriving in Rosslare Harbour. The vessel has 2 restaurants, bars and lounges, plus a children's free cinema and a "Cyber Zone" with electronic games and entertainment. During the summer period there is a live entertainment programme onboard, also a Tourist Information Centre giving information on South Wales and South East Ireland. Throughout the year we offer low cost Day Trips for visitors to the area, and early spring or autumn moneysaving offers for passengers with cars. Irish Ferries Holidays also have a great choice of inclusive short and long break holidays in hotels, self catering and motoring holidays for all the family throughout Ireland.

INDEX

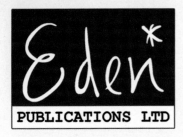

Eden Publications Ltd
3 Lords Meadow View
Pembroke, SA71 4BA
Tel/Fax: 01646 682296
Mob: 07971703599
Website: www.edenpublications.co.uk
Email: info@edenpublications.co.uk

Here at Eden Publications Ltd we offer a full Design and Printing Service. Whether you are are interested in having a Bespoke Postcard made, Leaflets or Flyers printed, Brochures published, any form of Stationery designed, we can handle the job.

If it's printed, we can design it and print it

BESPOKE POSTCARDS, LEAFLETS, FLYERS BROCHURES, COMPLIMENT SLIPS BUSINESS CARDS, STATIONERY PROMOTIONAL MATERIAL

We also have an extensive digital photographic library to suit all of your publishing needs. Our vast catalogue covers all of Pembrokeshire and reaches into Ceredigion. We only use the best equipment and we are constantly updating our library.

We also offer a full Photography Service, if you are putting together a new Brochure for your business then why not use our professional service to ensure the best quality images possible.